LEAN CULTURE
THE LEADER'S GUIDE

WHAT YOU NEED TO KNOW AND
DO TO IMPLEMENT LEAN CULTURE
IN YOUR ORGANIZATION

Lawrence M. Miller

COPYRIGHT

LAWRENCE M. MILLER

ANNAPOLIS, MARYLAND, 2011
LMMILLER@LMMILLER.COM
WWW.LMMILLER.COM

ISBN # 978-0-578-07584-6

1. Organizational Effectiveness. 2. Leadership. 3. Organization
Culture. 4. Corporate Culture. 5. Change Management

This book is available at quantity discounts from the
author. Please contact him at the above email address.

Published by

LMMiller
Publishing

CONTENTS

PREFACE

Lean management and culture has become the standard setting model of modern management. However, effective management did not begin and will not end with what we now think of as *lean*. Many previous methods and theories have contributed to today's best practices. If you are managing a business you are too busy to sort out all the hype around various techniques and buzz words. I have tried to help by integrating best practices into a single unified process that deals with both the habits of daily life in the organization and a more strategic view of developing organizational capabilities.

When Shoichiro Irimajiri came to the United States to lead the startup of Honda America Manufacturing in Marysville, Ohio he happened to buy a book in the Tokyo airport before his flight. This book, *American Spirit: Visions of a New Corporate Culture*, proposed that there were eight cultural principles inherent in the American culture upon which a new corporate culture could be build. "Mr. Iri", as Irimajiri would come to be known, thought that "If this is what Americans believe, we can succeed." This book was then used in the training of all of Honda's managers for some time. Scott Whitlock, the Executive Vice President of Honda America Manufacturing, taught the course on the Honda Way. He would periodically call me to clarify some obscure point in my book that I had completely forgotten about!

Several times I went to Honda to study their culture and speak to their managers and suppliers. What was clear was that Honda was not simply copying what they had done in Japan. They were not focused on any one method or technique. They were creative pragmatists. They were carefully adapting American cultural principles to their own and synthesizing the best of both worlds. They had a firm dedication to principles and a belief that those principles had to be lived by all associates at every level of the organization. Mr. Iri was himself a model of the behavior and the culture he was trying to build. They were just as focused on creating the optimum social system as they were the technical system or work flow. The leadership he provided was not imitative, but creative. It was not something delegated to others, but was his personal mission.

What I am proposing to you in this book is that you adopt a similar approach. Respect and learn from what others have done. Model the principles and behavior you seek in others – be the change! And, be creative. Thoughtfully design the organizational systems and structures, social and technical, which support and reinforce your desired culture. This is the hard work of lean leadership.

This book is divided into two parts: Part One is a strategic process to align the organization to lean culture. Think of it this way – a culture of democracy cannot exist without the systems and structures that enable democracy. Most of the systems and structures of your organization were created in a previous culture, based on that culture's assumptions and values. They reinforce and sustain the old culture, not the new one. They must be reconsidered and aligned to reinforce the behavior you want now and in the future. Part One provides an outline of a process to align your organization to lean culture. This is the job of leaders!

Part Two is about "being the change." Lean is a culture of continuous improvement at every level of the organization. If the daily habits of continuous improvement are to be instituted as the normal way of life in your organization, you must be the change, model the behavior. The importance of modeling the behavior you desire cannot be overemphasized. Many lean implementations focus on techniques on the shop floor and fail to address the behavior and daily practices of managers. This is the primary cause of failure.

Part Two is drawn from my training manual, *Lean Team Management* and presents the core material on building an effective lean management team without the accompanying exercises and some of the skill building material.

I have also included two additional chapters that present what I believe to be useful perspectives on strategic leadership.

INTRODUCTION

What is Lean Culture?

Lean culture is a lot more than tools and techniques like JIT, 5S, or value-stream mapping. It is the framework of values, daily habits and relationships within which those techniques can succeed and be sustained. It is the daily management process. It is the internal strategy of the firm. Without the support of the culture, lean techniques often fail. The sustainable value is in the culture and management process in which continuous improvement becomes a daily habit at every level. Building this culture is the purpose of this book.

Lean culture is not one thing. No one can authoritatively state "This is it, and nothing more!" The culture of Toyota and Honda are not the same. The culture of FEDEX and Intel are not the same. The culture of lean manufacturing organizations and lean healthcare organizations are not the same.

Two things are true: first, there are common principles that are being applied to develop lean organizations. And second, all great companies are constantly innovating, moving and not standing still. Lean is a learning organization.

Lean is not blindly copying what someone else has done. Lean is first understanding principles and examples from other companies, and then seeking to apply those principles to your own environment. Lean is innovating. Lean is continuous improvement.

LEAN CULTURE IS...

- The engagement of all members of the organization, from top-to-bottom in a consistent and organized process of continuous improvement in both processes and people.
- Leadership that understands, practices, models and reinforces the values and behavior of lean culture. Be the change!
- A culture in which the leaders both respect and encourage those who are on-the-spot and "the world's greatest experts" in their work.
- The elimination of all forms of waste, non-value-adding things and activities, including wasteful management activity.
- The continuous effort to optimize quality of products, services and processes.

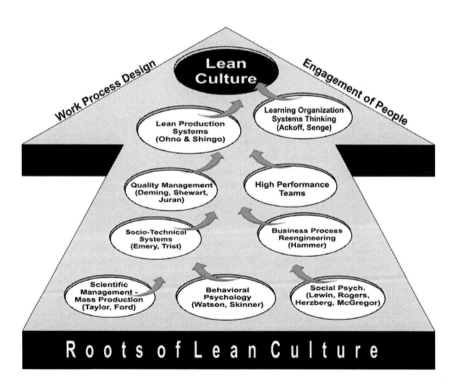

THE ROOTS OF LEAN CULTURE

This author has been involved in organization development efforts of many varieties for about thirty-five years. Long before anyone thought of the word "lean" and before Toyota was considered to be a model organization, earlier pioneers were developing and studying the design of high performing organizations, developing systems of engaging employees, scientifically studying reward and recognition systems, and researching various problem-solving techniques. The Toyota Production System incorporated and benefited from many of these earlier efforts. Lean management has incorporated many lessons learned by pioneers like Dr. Deming, Fred Emery and Eric Trist, Skinner, Herzberg, McGregor, Ackoff, Senge and dozens of others.

Those who are new to organization development tend to think that the technique, model or buzz word of the day is the Holy Grail without realizing the flow, the history of learning that led us to where we are. There is also a misunderstanding that a collection of lean tools equals lean culture. Culture is not tools. This often leads to a failure of understanding, a fanaticism about today's technique, and unwillingness to explore, improve and move forward. A perspective of historical development creates humility and humility is the first prerequisite for learning.

From the preceding diagram an entire book could be written and an entire semester of a college course on organization development structured. That is not our purpose here. Yet, it will help to understand lean culture and methods of change if one has some appreciation for the roots upon which lean culture has emerged.

RETURN TO THE FAMILY FARM

There is one critical understanding about human motivation and the organization of work that is essential to an understanding of lean culture. This is an understanding of how we have transitioned from a million years of working in small groups, the hunting party, the family farm and craft shop, to mass production, and now to lean production.

The family system was the first work group, and families are the foundation building block of every society, every civilization, in every corner of the globe. We don't do many useful things by ourselves. Hunting antelope on the Serengeti plains or hunting Buffalo in the American West was a team survival sport. Hunting alone would lead to starvation. To be expelled from your group, your family or tribe, meant death. Working in groups is in our genetic code. It is linked to our survival as a species.

The family farm was a work and social system based on high intimacy, high trust, and high ownership of the work. Psychological and social needs were well met by this system. That is why it lasted for hundreds of thousands of years. But the invention of the combine and the tractor drastically improved efficiency on the farm and now required less labor. Labor moved to the cities to work in the large factories and now everything changed.

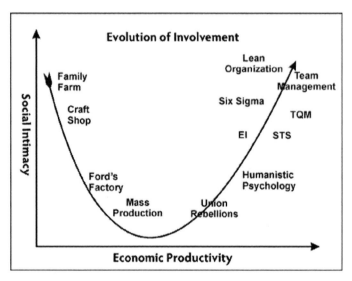

The mass production model of Henry Ford's factory increased productivity but destroyed intimacy. Units produced relative to hours of work went up dramatically due to the innovations of mass production. We gained economic efficiency and productivity, but with that system, we sacrificed social intimacy and psychological security. Workers didn't make a whole car as they made a whole piece of furniture in a craft shop. Work was simplified and specialized to the point where workers were told to "do your own work" and not think about the work of others. Workers were socially and psychologically isolated.

In the inner city, when the family structure is falling apart, young people form gangs. And, they call each other "brother" and "sister." You may think that there is a "gang problem" but the reality is that the gang is the solution to the problem. Human beings require bonding with others, the psychological safety of a small group. When mass production organizations created psychological isolation the workers organized and called each other "brother" and "sister." They were fulfilling a psychological necessity.

But, now we are smarter. We know that we must create organizations that do not isolate individuals, but rather create natural small group organizations, that fulfill the same need as was fulfilled by the family farm and craft shop. Intimacy and efficiency can be combined and this is what lean culture has done. Throughout this book you will see the word "team." When you see "team" think "family farm;" think the basic family structure that is the source of learning, values and psychological security in every culture. You may call your groups work cells or some other name. It doesn't matter. The key thing is that you build your organization on small groups who are engaged in learning, who know their customers, are empowered to make decisions and improve their process.

THE TEN CULTURAL CHARACTERISTICS OF LEAN ORGANIZATIONS

High performing organizations are not all the same. Yet, there are common cultural characteristics, principles that can be applied to any organization in the pursuit of lean or high performance. The following ten principles are all about ***engaging all members of the organization in teamwork focused on continuous improvement of the work processes that serve customers***. This is the over-arching cultural principle.

THE POWER OF PURPOSE

Lean organizations instill a high level motivation in their members. This begins with a fundamental understanding of their purpose.

There are many sources of motivation and we do not all have the same needs. However, at our core, deep in our soul, we have something in common. We all need to feel a sense of meaning in our lives, a purpose to which we will dedicate ourselves. We find purpose in many ways – in our faith, our community and our family. Leaders lead by instilling a sense of noble purpose in their followers. Purpose creates energy; the manager can then provide guidance and direction to that energy. But absent the energy, absent the sense of purpose, management becomes extremely difficult.

Organizations motivate people in many ways, but they must start with an understanding of the human need for purpose. Purpose can be to heal the sick, to provide healthy and satisfying entertainment, to make a safe and reliable car, or to create software that maximizes human learning and understanding. Purpose is the beginning of strategy.

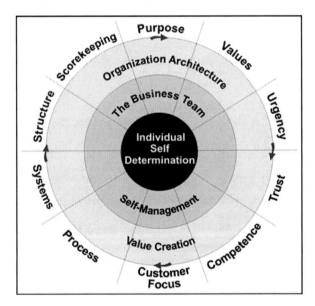

The mandate of each team in the organization can be linked to the larger purpose of the organization. The shipping team understands their impact on customer perceptions of responsiveness and reliability. The engineering team understands their impact on safety, reliability and customer satisfaction. These connections are a unifying element that reduce conflicts and increase the ability of the organization to "win" as one large team.

VALUES – THE KNOWLEDGE OF TRUE NORTH

Strong families and communities are characterized by strong values. Values simply define "right" conduct. In the United States we have cultural values that respect freedom of speech and religion and obedience to law. In your home and through your faith you learned the value of "doing unto others as you would have them do onto you." These are very simple ideas. Yet, the degree to which we practice these simple ideas largely defines the strength of our family and community. The same is true within the organization.

The importance of values in organizations has seen its ups and downs. There was a day when Henry Ford would only hire "good Christian men" as his expression of the importance he placed on the trustworthiness of his workers. We have worked with clients such as Chick-fil-A where meetings often start with a prayer and at the entrance to the headquarters building is the announcement "Dedicated to the Glory of God." While these overtly religious expressions may not be acceptable in every organization, we have learned the hard way the importance of strong values in preserving the integrity and economic value of a business.

Values are important not only to avoid scandals, but also to drive and direct behavior that impacts economic performance. Going back to the simple efforts of Benjamin Franklin to hold himself accountable each day for one of his thirteen virtues and more recent "principle-centered" leadership, we have seen the connection between how individuals, teams and organizations achieve results while pursuing their beliefs. Values are the social glue that unites people. Defining and instilling values is the essential task of all leaders.

URGENCY: THE PASSION FOR IMPROVEMENT

I spent several days in one of the world's best lean organizations and a week later I spent several days in another organization that was deeply troubled and had not begun its journey toward becoming a lean organization. As I sat in on the management meetings at one organization I felt an incredible sense of urgency. In the other organization the managers seemed very relaxed and as they spoke about problems it seemed that the cause of those problems was outside the organization and they did not feel an urgency to change things.

As you may imagine, it was the highly successful organization that felt the urgency to improve and the poor organization where the managers seemed to feel that things were not that bad. At first glance, this seems to be a strange distortion of reality. One would think it should have been the other way around. Yet the fact is that the passion to improve at a high speed, the "racing spirit" at Honda, is the cause of excellence. Those who are excellent, both individuals and organizations, are in rapid motion. The sense of comfort or ease is a sign of a culture in decline.

I believe in the power of free will. Many years ago when working in the prisons of North Carolina, I realized that almost all of the inmates sincerely believed that someone else – the "other guys" – were responsible for their incarceration. Some other guy had talked them into it. Another "other guy", the lawyer, had failed to do his job. The judge was biased against him. To say the least, these inmates were not good learners. They did not process feedback or reflect on their own responsibility. They saw themselves as victims.

In psychology there is a concept of "locus-of-control", a continuum from internality to externality. Locus-of-control is about where we place responsibility for the events in our life, inside us, under our control, or outside of us, on the "other guys." My inmates were a good sample of externals and the extreme of what happens to externals – they tend to lose. All excellent executives and entrepreneurs I have ever known have had a belief in their own ability to make things happen, their responsibility, their ability to control the events in their life. They were internals.

Woody Allen said eighty percent of success is showing up. I would modify that to say that eighty percent of success is showing up with urgency and a belief that you can change things. And that energy comes from your acceptance of challenge and the recognition that success is in your hands.

TRUST – THE POWER OF SOCIAL CAPITAL

The ability to work together, to solve problems, depends on trusting relationships between colleagues. This social capital is a cultural characteristic of growing economies as well as companies: Some companies, with apparent ease, attract and retain the best people. Some companies, almost effortlessly, promote continual learning and the sharing of knowledge. Some appear to be more a network of social, collegial relationships, than an organization at all. Some companies have relationships with customers and suppliers that extend over decades. It is worth considering that all economic activity is based on social relationships. These relationships represent an asset, what may be called social capital.

A recent book by Francis Fukuyama presents a well thought out argument that "one of the most important lessons we can learn from an examination of economic life is that a nation's well-being, as well as its ability to compete, is conditioned by a single, pervasive cultural characteristic: the level of trust inherent in the society." [1]   High-trust societies are more successful at wealth creation. Those which are low-trust societies demonstrate less ability to generate material wealth. Low-trust societies, such as those in the Middle East, extend trust within, but little beyond, the family association. This lack of trust acts as a brake on economic activity.

The same process takes place within the mini-society of the corporation. Leaders who create trust encourage shared learning, open discussion of problems and possible improvements, and freely share information. Just as a free and democratic society is an "open society" based on social capital that creates wealth, so the corporation must become an "open society" that values social capital and creates other forms of wealth that are linked to that social capital.

The question then becomes, how do our processes, our systems, our training, and our leadership practices promote effective relationships and trust? Building this trust is one of the essential goals of lean culture.

COMPETENCY: THE CHAIN OF CAPABILITY

---

[1] Fukuyama, Francis: Trust: The Social Virtues & The Creation of Prosperity, New York, The Free Press, 1995.

Lean organizations are smart organizations. Of course, organizations are neither smart nor dumb. It is people who are smart. It is people who must strive to be the world's greatest experts in their work. High performing organizations invest in and value personal development and knowledge at every level and in every function. Leadership must convey and reinforce the value of the continual pursuit of competence.

Most performance in the work place requires competence, not mere knowledge. You may *know* how to play the violin, but does that knowledge equal the *skill* to perform with excellence? No. You may have read books on selling skills but not translated that knowledge into genuine competence at selling. You may have read books on group decision-making and facilitation, but that does not necessarily translate into performance. Competence is the ability to perform, and it requires knowledge, plus practice, feedback and reflection. This is the cycle of human development, and the best companies manage the development of competency.

Individuals may possess competence in technical skills and social skills. Technical skills include the operation of machinery as well as the technical work done by a finance or marketing team. Social skills include the skills of working in teams, problem-solving, and decision-making. Capability resides in the organization's ability to chain these competencies together in a process that is able to achieve desired results. The capability to design an automobile and get it into production within a short cycle is a capability of the organization. But many different sets of individual competencies are required to accomplish the task. The capability to discover drugs or to design new software is an organizational capability comprised of dozens of competencies. It is the job of the leadership team to identify the strategic capabilities required to achieve business success. It is the job of human resource development to identify the necessary competencies required to achieve those organizational capabilities.

CUSTOMER FOCUS: A PASSION FOR SERVING OTHERS

Each management theory makes a contribution to our value stream of knowledge. Dr. Deming and other quality management gurus rightfully promoted a "passion for customers." This made a lasting change in the culture of our corporations. Lean extends this passion in a systematic process of a chain of teams, aligned horizontally through the organization, each with defined customers and suppliers, and each given responsibility to manage and continuously improve the process that serves their customers.

Often, the customer focus we see is more passionate where companies interface with the end-use customer who writes a check. That is understandable. But one of the most distinguishing characteristics of lean organizations is the ability to create a customer focused culture at every step in the process. Every team has customers. High performance teams have a passionate recognition of their direct customers, internal or external, and measure their performance in terms of customer satisfaction.

PROCESS OWNERSHIP: THE BUSINESS OF THE TEAM

Dr. Deming used to say that "98% of the quality problems are in the process, but 98% of the time we blame the person and fail to fix the process." Whether he was right about his percentages doesn't matter. His point is a very valid one. It is much easier to blame an individual rather than do the hard work of improving the process. Of course improvement will also come by enhancing personal competence. However, if the normal way we do things is inherently ineffective, the individual will soon become de-motivated as she attempts to overcome the obstacles created by a poor process.

There are micro and macro processes in every organization. It is the job of leaders to assure that every process is owned by some individual or team. Process ownership and accountability is key to lean culture.

SYSTEMS THAT SUPPORT

In the human body, the system of veins, arteries and nerves, enables every limb and organ to act in a coordinated and purposeful manner. If these systems fail to function, every limb and organ of the body fails. Similarly, organizations are dependent on the flow of information and money, the systems of training and development, the systems of motivation and evaluation, and the process of feedback and scorekeeping.

Systems must be aligned to support those who own and manage the core work process. In many organizations the current systems have been designed on principles and assumption at variance with those of lean culture.

I was taking my first tour of a manufacturing plant that had become our client. We were given the assignment to change the culture, improve quality and implement a system of total employee involvement. As I toured the plant with the plant manager I asked him about the employee compensation system. He said that I didn't need to worry about that because he had another consultant who worked on the compensation system. I said "Yes, but it may affect how the teams perform. What is the system of compensation?"

He then told me that everyone was on "piece-rate," individual incentives determined by individual jobs and individual performance. But, we weren't supposed to worry about that while we attempted to implement a work-team structure with teams focused on the performance of the group and their process. Not likely! This is misalignment of systems. It is obvious that change is more difficult when different systems point in different directions and create conflict and tension within the individual.

Aligning the system to the strategy, structure, and processes of the organization is one of the critical steps in creating lean culture.

STRUCTURES THAT ENABLE FLOW

Structure matters – walls, levels, divisions, like the canyons and tall building of our cities, separate us into "mine" and "yours" and obstruct a view of the horizon. The easy sociability of genuine community is interrupted by walls that separate us. The walls are between departments or other groupings that interrupt the actual flow of work. The purpose of structure is to enable the flow of the work, not to interrupt it. But, this must be deliberately designed.

As the culture of organizations evolves, so too must organizational structure. Over the past twenty years we have made a rapid transition from the assumptions of hierarchically and functionally based organization to the assumptions of organizing around processes and networks of individuals with common interests. However, as we have dramatically changed our processes, the alignment of structure has often been left behind.

Many organizations today wish to focus on the horizontal processes but are still held back by hierarchical structures and the walls between departments. Many teams, given training and instructions to be more self-managing, are held back by managers whose role definitions have not adapted to the new culture. New culture requires new structure. New structure requires new role definitions.

Some years ago my associates and I were working with Clark-Schwebel, a high technology textile manufacturing company in South Carolina and Georgia. Ricky Wolf, the Vice President of Manufacturing and I were touring the four manufacturing facilities to introduce the concept high performance teams and flatter organization. We held a meeting with all management and supervision in the cafeteria of one of the plants. I did my usual talk about teamwork and the new culture. Ricky Wolf then got up and announced that by the time we were through designing the new system everyone in the room would lose their job. I sat their gasping and thinking "Oh no! Everyone is going to hate us from the start!" He then said, "But, no one will lose employment. Every job will change. There will be new jobs with new roles and responsibilities. There will be no supervisors as you have always understood that role. There will be *team leaders* who will support, facilitate and lead the work of teams." Then I could breathe again! This little speech had a terrifically positive affect. They got it. New culture equals new roles and responsibilities.

The answer to improved performance is rarely, if ever, to be found simply in the structure of organizations. Yet, structures can significantly hinder the ability of individuals and groups to perform. It is our responsibility to design structures that will facilitate the processes of work and decision-making that will enhance performance.

KEEPING SCORE – PLAYING THE GAME

Imagine any environment in which individuals or teams put forth maximum effort, achieve maximum results, and have fun while they are at it. In such an environment you will find scorekeeping, immediate feedback, and visual display of the score. This is a simple and obvious thing. Why isn't it as common as it is obvious?

Beginning in the early 1970's I was involved in implementing performance improvement programs in manufacturing plants. The idea of graphing and charting performance, visually displaying the ups and downs of a team's performance was a new thing in most manufacturing plants. Virtually every time performance was visually graphed for a team to see its own performance, performance improved. It is the "no-brainer" of performance improvement. Blitz almost any group with feedback and performance will improve. Simplistic? Yes, but effective. Everything that works doesn't have to be complicated.

Scorekeeping has gone through numerous iterations and fads. From the Management by Objectives of the 1950s and 60s to the currently fashionable Six Sigma version of quality management, there have been numerous techniques that have derived much of their power from the simple impact of visual feedback and knowledge of performance.

Every business manager is driven by the "game" of business, watching sales scores, costs and the competition. In many ways owning a company and being a business manager is fun. It is fun, not because of the actual work, but because of the game, the scoreboard, the wins and losses. Why can't every employee experience the same joy of the game? They can. The purpose of business teams is to be the structure, the vehicle, by which every individual in the organization has the opportunity to play the business game.

PART ONE

INTERNAL STRATEGY:

ALIGNING THE ORGANIZATION TO

LEAN CULTURE

CHAPTER *1*

THE FIVE S'S OF LEAN CULTURE
SYSTEMS, STRUCTURE, SYMBOLS,
SKILLS AND STYLE

There is no "one right way" to develop the culture of an organization. However, there is a great deal of research and field experience that point to some clear lessons.

The first lesson, one on which everyone with experience will agree, is that changing the culture requires strong and constant leadership from those who hold real power in the organization. This cannot be some "do good for a day", lip service effort. The leaders must understand that the culture is a, or the, primary source of competitive advantage – a requirement for strategic business success. This is the starting point. If the leaders cannot get their heads behind this – just stop here.

In order for the implementation of lean culture to succeed it must be aligned with business strategy and objectives. Just as TQM, high performance teams, and many other change efforts failed if they were not understood as a means to achieve business results, the link between lean culture and business success and survival must be clear in everyone's mind. It is the job of the leaders to create this clear, line of sight relationship between business results and any improvement effort.

Lean culture implies significant alteration of values for many organizations. For example, at Honda you will frequently hear the

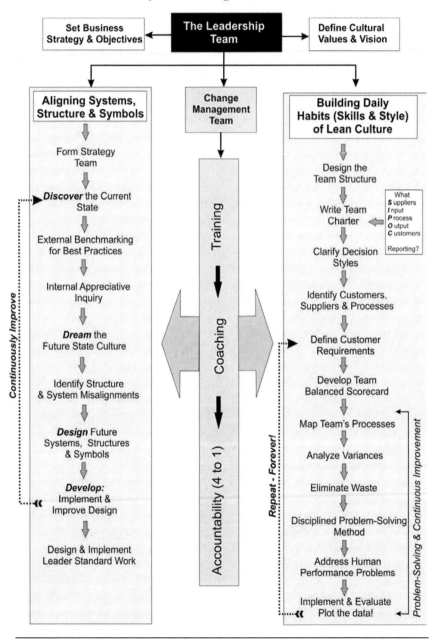

Implementing Lean Culture

phrase "the world's greatest experts are on-the-spot." This phrase is a statement of values. Because of this value, even a newly hired and experienced public relations manager is asked to spend weeks working on manufacturing teams so that she can "learn respect for those who are on-the-spot."

Change starts with an understanding and commitment to values upon which behavior, systems, structure and symbols will all be built. Defining these values is the beginning of internal strategy and it is the task of the leadership team.

Most organizations will find it helpful to have a designated change management team comprised of individuals who have expertise in lean management and organization development. This team is most often comprised of one external change agent, a group of internal coaches and several key line managers. The task of this change management team is to provide overall direction to the specific process of change and to provide feedback to the leadership team. They will plan training, coaching and accountability, with an emphasis on the positive appreciation of good efforts and improvements, rather than pointing out failures. The Four-to-One rule applies.

The change effort can then be divided into two major tracks of activity. One is focused on behavior change, a change in the daily habits of how we work and manage. The second is focused on aligning the systems, structures and symbols of the organization to support the new culture. Most of this book, and the *Lean Team Management* workbook, are focused on developing the daily habits, the skills and style of lean culture. The rest of this chapter defines the Five S's and the next two chapters outline a process of aligning these to the new culture.

THE KEY PILLARS OF CULTURE

When the United States Constitution was written it included statements of intention... freedom of speech and religion, equal protection of the law and others. Yet these statements alone did not make those aspirations real in the lives of all citizens. In many ways, the culture of the country was far behind the aspiration. It required a long series of legislative efforts, and enforcement of law, to bring the culture in line with the intentions of the founding document. Similarly in corporations, changing the culture requires clear decisions regarding its structure and systems that create the mechanisms that support desired culture.

Changing the culture means changing "real stuff" that drives behavior. One way of addressing these is to address the 5S's of lean culture – **Structure, Systems, Skills, Style** and **Symbols**. These five S's should not be confused with the 5S's that are most often promoted in lean manufacturing. Those deal with orderliness in the work setting. While those are important, they do not address the most important things that drive the culture. The five S's that follow are the pillars that hold up and support the culture. Aligning these to the desired culture is the job of management.

STRUCTURE:

There is an apparent organic process of growth in the structure and complexity of companies. An entrepreneurial company starts out with a simple structure: folks who make stuff and folks who sell stuff. Soon they have support groups of finance, HR and others. With growth, each of these subdivides and additional groups are added. All of these are needed, up to a point.

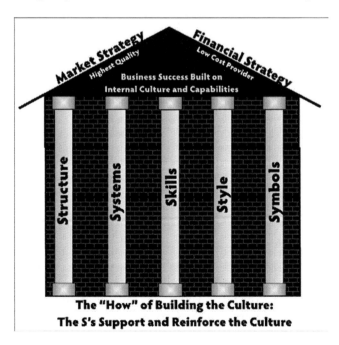

The "How" of Building the Culture:
The S's Support and Reinforce the Culture

But the moment of growth in structure almost inevitably goes too far, creating a bureaucracy that hinders the important work that serves customers.

Bureaucracy is an excess and inflexibility of structure. It slows down decisions, slows down work processes, and dis-empowers both managers and employees from making decisions.

I have had a good deal of success redesigning organization structures from the bottom up, around the work process. In other words, you begin by defining the ideal work flow through the organization. You then design the structure from the bottom-up, starting with the first level teams, with the criteria of enabling and optimizing the work process. The purpose of structure should be to enhance the flow of the work and avoid creating inhibitors, walls, silos and unnecessary levels that will inevitably stifle creativity and improvement.

The more layers of management in an organization, the less likely that those at the first level will be empowered to make significant decisions. Each layer draws decision-making authority and responsibility up and away from those with their hands on the real work. A lean culture is a culture of self-management in which employees are responsible for the quality of their work. The structure must facilitate this self-management.

SYSTEMS:

If you think of the construction of a house you can see the structure of walls, foundation, roof, floors, etc. But the construction of a house requires much more. The quality of life in the house will largely be determined by the systems that run through the walls: the heating and air condition, electrical wires, wires to support Internet access and security systems. These systems bring life to an otherwise dead structure.

Systems in organizations serve a similar function. They define much of the life in the organization. Organizations maintain efficiency and sanity through dozens of systems: hiring, discipline, firing, communication, training, compensation, recognition, promotion, etc. Without systems every event would be treated as unique and require a separate judgment. Chaos would result.

Lean culture requires systems that are designed to support that culture. How will employees be hired, trained, motivated, disciplined, and promoted? The design of each of these systems reflects cultural assumptions about the role and importance of people in the organization. Who does the hiring? Managers only, or are team members involved? What are the competencies and qualities by which you judge potential employees? What is included in new employee orientation? What resources are devoted to training?

There are dozens of questions regarding the human resource and information systems that should be answered in a way that will reinforce the desired culture. In most organizations these systems are designed by individuals who may be expert in their area, but who lack an understanding of the connection between these systems and culture. Those who design information systems may be very good at their work, but are they designing the flow of information to enable work teams to take responsibility and make decisions on-the-spot? Are they designing real-time visual feedback for those doing value adding work? Probably not.

One of the first efforts to redesign organizations to optimize performance was the work of Fred Emery and Eric Trist. They developed a methodology that was known as *socio-technical systems* design, or STS. The first manufacturing plants in the United States to incorporate self-managing teams were designed according to STS methodology. This methodology presumed that those who did the work, who were "on-the-spot," knew best what they needed to accomplish the work. This methodology was first used at the Gaines Topeka pet food plant and later at all Proctor and Gamble plants. My firm took this technology and merged it with TQM thinking and methods.

It is useful to think about all the systems and practices in organizations that are technical or social systems. These are often designed separately and not designed as a whole system. This creates misalignment. They should be designed together. Many lean efforts fail because they focus on technical systems and fail to understand how they are dependent on social systems.

The following systems enable the workflow and may be designed to provide optimum support for that value stream.

- *Organization structure* has only one legitimate purpose: to enable the core work of the organization that serves customers and produces revenue. Any structures that do not contribute to this core work or inhibit the work are waste. Structure should be designed from the bottom up.

- *Human resource systems* should also be designed with an understanding of the requirements of the core work process and to facilitate or enhance that process. The goal of these systems should be to optimize the competencies and motivation that will enhance the return on capital.

- *Internal and external communications* support the creation of trust and reinforce the values and purpose of the organization.

- *Information systems* should be designed to enhance the ownership and control of the associates who are on-the-spot doing the value adding work as well as to keep management informed.

- *Financial systems*, in addition to informing management of progress toward financial goals, should also enable teams to evaluate the progress of their own work toward eliminating waste and satisfying customer desires.

SKILLS:

Human competence is the essential capital of competent organizations. The ability of an organization to develop the skills of its members is likely to determine its long-term success.

The effort to create lean culture must plan for all of the skills and knowledge necessary to meet the requirements of current processes that serve current customers, and future processes that will serve future customers. A competency model should be defined for each significant position in the organization. What competencies are required for a plant manager, a manufacturing manager, a first level team leader, and for each other position. The competency model should define minimal critical specifications and desired or optimal specifications. The training and development process should be built on this competency model, to bring individuals to the desired level of competence for the current position and for positions to which they may be promoted.

This definition should include both **technical** and **people skills**. Technical skills should include operating equipment, specialized knowledge in mechanics, chemistry, sales, or any other function of the individual or team. The people skills may also be called social or management skills. These would include training skills, team facilitation, problem-solving, or any other skills relating to the ability of people to work together.

STYLE:

The character of day-to-day interactions among the members of an organization is that organization's style. Style is behavior, the specific behaviors of how we communicate and convey values, judgments, and priorities. The style of managers is inevitably linked to the structure and systems but also to their functional skills and even the physical environment in which the work takes place.

Style has a significant impact on the ability of an organization to make effective decisions, motivate its employees, and bring about unified action. The style of managers can be clearly viewed in the group decision-making process. One manager with whom we worked claimed to be a great advocate of participative decision-making. He said all the right things. In group meetings he would proclaim loudly that he wanted everyone to speak their mind and that, "This is a group decision." None of his managers were ever comfortable with or trusting of these proclamations. After observing his behavior or his style in the group, the reason for their disbelief was well founded. When he stated his view, he did so with an intimidating tone of voice that signaled to everyone in the room that there was only one right decision. When contrary views were stated, the very movement of his eyes made the mistake clear. His style dominated his own good intentions and stifled the participative process.

This manager needed coaching. He was not a bad person, was not ignorant, and wanted to do the right things. But his habitual patterns of behavior contradicted his good intentions. When implementing lean culture it is very helpful to have a process of coaching each manager as they seek to improve.

SYMBOLS:

We value rational judgment and behavior. We look down upon other cultures with their rituals and symbolic gestures as something of the past. Yet, if we could see ourselves through the eyes of an archaeologist 1000 years hence, we might have quite a different perspective. Picking through the ruins of a once tall office building, our future archaeologist might find strange pieces of cloth tied around the necks of each male who was surrounded by other symbols of the decision-making class. The archeologist knew who was of that class because of their private offices, ritualistic in size and furnishing. He might attempt to develop a theory that the piece of cloth tied around the neck was used to signal approval or disapproval in the decision-making process. Perhaps he might theorize that it was slung over one shoulder to signal approval and the other to signal disapproval. Surely knowing what a rational society we had developed, he would assume that it possessed some functional value. Or would he look down upon us and assume that we were so irrational as to obey ritualistically customs to which we could ascribe no useful function (waste)?

We employ all sorts of symbols in ritualistic fashion, and like the inhabitants of other cultures, give little thought to their origin or their impact on behavior. Some companies have separate parking and entrances for managers. Why? Is it to send a message that managers are different, superior to, and more important than everyone else? Why do we want to send this message? The president of Honda America Manufacturing sits in his "office," a large room with dozens of other identical desks and with other employees all dressed like him, in a white smock-like uniform. Can he not afford a private office? Does he not understand that familiarity breeds contempt, and therefore he should not mingle so closely with his employees? Honda performs quite well despite this violation of the traditions of American corporate culture. Honda regards the principle of "Unity" and "Consensus" very seriously. They train their managers in these principles and have designed their culture to promote the spirit of unity and consensus.

Symbols are generally not important unto themselves. Whether the president of Honda has a private office or whether there are reserved parking places for managers has little impact on the bottom line of the company. It is the teaching impact of symbols that is important. It is the messages they communicate which changes behavior and impact results. In the southern United States not too many years ago, there were separate water fountains for "White" and "Colored." The same water flowed into each so some said, "What's the big deal?" The importance of separate water fountains was the message of a culture that taught that the two classes and colors were not equal. Symbols communicate, and the communication was clear. The symbols had to be changed to change the process of learning and all the subsequent judgments and behavior that followed from that learning.

It has been my experience that changing symbols can be among the most powerful and important decisions a design team makes. While many perceive these as unimportant they communicate powerful messages of change to the organization. The greater population of employees is often looking for some symbolic changes to demonstrate a real change in the culture of the organization.

CHAPTER *2*

LEAN CULTURE AND CAPABILITY STRATEGY:

The purpose of this chapter is to provide a framework for developing internal (culture and capabilities) strategy that will enable external (market and financial) strategy. Creating the best possible company, your ideal organization, requires long term and holistic strategy that results in specific and concrete actions by all managers and employees.

Most corporations have strategic plans and a strategic planning process. And the focus of these plans is generally on two things: market strategy and financial strategy. Market strategy focuses on what products or services will we produce, with what features, to meet which market segments. This requires an analysis of market trends, pricing patterns in different segments, and trends in technology. Financial strategy establishes targets for revenue, margins, costs and return to shareholders. Both of these components of strategy are necessary, but not sufficient. What are often not defined are the internal capabilities that will be required to achieve the desired market and financial targets.

Imagine that a company decides on a strategy to enter and win the Formula One World Championship. They set targets for the number of races they will win, the advertising income they will receive and the measures of customer recognition or brand value that they will achieve. This is their external strategy. What about internal strategy? What human talents, competencies and motivation will be required? What types of innovation will be needed to compete against the other Formula One teams? What driver and engineering capabilities are required? What is their plan for developing driver skills? Without effectively answering these questions about internal capabilities and culture, the external strategy is no strategy at all, it is merely strategic wishing!

INTERNAL STRATEGY: CULTURE AND CAPABILITIES

Stephen Covey wrote that "If you want to make minor, incremental changes and improvements, work on practices, behavior or attitudes. But if you want to make significant, quantum improvements, work on paradigms."[2] Internal strategy is about choosing your paradigms and principles and then aligning the organization to those.

Culture and capabilities are the assets, the productive, value adding assets held by an organization. If you had zero money, but if you had a team of dedicated scientists who knew how to cure cancer, you would be in possession of an incredibly valuable asset. Yet, it would not appear on the balance sheet or be visible in cash flow. Similarly, what has distinguished Honda and Toyota and companies like Intel, Apple and Facebook, is their human abilities to generate innovation that will be appreciated by customers, result in brand loyalty and new revenue.

THE GOAL: TO CREATE AND SUSTAIN WEALTH

What is wealth? What are the valuable assets of a person or organization? We think of money, but money is not in the beginning. The word, the creative spirit, purpose and values, are in the beginning. The cycle of wealth begins with a creative act of leadership that inspires unity of energy and effort. The ideas, the creative spirit, purpose and values - spiritual capital - come first. This then generates the wealth of social and human capital that stimulates innovation capital and finally results in financial capital.

---

[2] Covey, Stephen R. *The 8th Habit*. Free Press, New York, 2004. P. 19.

You may think of a house to illustrate the cultural assets of the organization. Each of these must be defined in a way that will contribute strategic advantage for the organization.

The Strategy Deployment House

Assets and Liabilities:
The "What" of Economic Success

SPIRITUAL CAPITAL:

To the degree that an organization can enable, support, or encourage a depth of personal morality and dedication to a noble purpose, it possesses spiritual capital. I sincerely believe that this form of wealth accrues both to the organization and to the individual. It will interact and support every other form of capital and ultimately will have its effect on the financial bottom line. In many ways it is the *first cause.*

The pursuit of *worthy purpose* is the primary means of achieving *energy* in an organization. Human beings are energized by, and will sacrifice for, that which they believe to be noble and therefore ennobling of them. Leaders create energy that may later be directed by managers, but absent the energy that comes from a worthy purpose, there is little motion. Any manager who believes that only technical processes, skills, or financial capital are required for competitive success is much like the racing team that spends a million dollars for the latest race car but then hires a driver who doesn't care about winning. Purpose matters. Ennobling purpose matters most.

Shared values are the basis for trustworthy relationships and sociability. Belief systems have enormous impact on the culture of organizations, and it is the function of leaders to exert efforts to intentionally shape these beliefs. A common set of values is the lubricant of fluid associations. It is the basis of unified action and trustworthy behavior. We trust those from our own family, community or religion; and have more difficulty trusting those from other families, communities or religions. This is because of our trust in their value system which predicts their behavior.

Complex societies, the world we live in today, force us to bridge trust across these natural boundaries. Corporations also require the building of trust across boundaries that might cause distrust in a simpler age. This bridging occurs by defining common values within the community of the corporation.

SOCIAL CAPITAL:

Social Capital is the value of trust. The degree of trust you engender in others will determine the likelihood of being hired, customers purchasing your products or services or, employees working and sacrificing for your company. It defines the likelihood that others will engage you in solving problems. It is a key to the effectiveness of all teams, families and communities. In the corporation it will determines innovation and brand equity. Entrepreneurs often begin their business within a small circle of trust and gradually expand the radius of trust, increasing the scope of their network and their business.

Social capital has been studied by the World Bank and economists who have demonstrated the correlation between "high trust" societies and economic growth. Sociability, the ability to form comfortable associations, is a requirement of economic activity. In low trust societies the "radius of trust" may extend only within families, limited by blood relationships. This is a break on economic activity. If sociability, or social capital, corresponds to successful economic activity in nations, it is reasonable that this is also true within corporations.

There are two types of social capital that may be assessed: internal sociability or trust, and external relationships or brand equity.

Internal social capital is the level of trust within the organization. Trust operates both horizontally and vertically within the organization and is critical to the ability to solve problems, innovate, and satisfy customers.

Internal sociability has its most significant impact on the ability to innovate and solve problems. All organizations are a continual stew of problem solving. Whether it is solving the problems presented by a customer, a new technology, or a competitor, business is a game of constant adaptation to a changing environment. The apparently small act of walking down the hall to an associate's office and sharing a problem, casually brainstorming without regard to who gets credit, or who bears what responsibility, is the most frequent, and probably the most effective way to solve problems. These encounters may escalate into a formal meeting or problem solving process. Whether the interaction remains highly informal or becomes more formal, the critical ingredient is the simple willingness to be engaged, to care about the problem, to listen deeply, think together, and brainstorm solutions.

External brand equity is the recognition and respect given to your firm by the market place. Just as the quality of an individual's life is largely determined by the quality of their social relationships, the same may be said of a company. The value of a company is directly related to its degree of trust in market place.

HUMAN CAPITAL:

Human capital is the sum of all of the competencies and motivation of the people within the organization. Human capital has always been a critical component of the performance of any business, but today's entrepreneur is likely to bring with him, not money, but competency and motivation, the two key ingredients of human capital. Attracting and retaining human capital will be one of the most critical challenges as a business grows.

Motivation has been the subject of hundreds, if not thousands of books for managers. When all is said and done, the keys to motivation are relatively simple: work that is interesting and ennobling; sincere recognition by peers and superiors; opportunities for career advancement; positive feedback that can guide performance; strong and supportive social interaction by a team; and, oh, did I forget? – fair and attractive financial rewards. There is little reason to waste time in the endless debates about which is more important: money, recognition, or enriching work. They are all motivating and different personalities are more or less influenced by different types of incentives. The job of designing an organizational system is to optimize all of the various forms of motivation. Over-reliance on any one form is a prescription for poor performance.

Human competence is the only modern parallel to production technology of the past century. Modern production most often occurs in the mind, or the collective mind of a small work group. If you have highly trained marketing professionals, skilled sales men and women, great engineers and brilliant financial managers, you have an important form of capital. These competencies are a foundation of performance. Investment in these assets is likely to pay off in the creation of other classes of assets.

Those organizations that have exhibited the greatest dedication to the development of human competence have consistently outperformed those who have only given lip service to training and development. General Electric, Microsoft, Toyota and other companies that have grown into great economic powers have done so as a result of both attracting and developing the most competent people.

INNOVATION CAPITAL:

Innovation grows in the soil of spiritual, social, and human capital. To the degree to which there is commitment to a worthy purpose, spiritual capital, members of the organization will engage in the discretionary effort of thinking, exercising their brain on a problem or opportunity. Many creative ideas occur on the weekend or in the evenings, when a member of your team is choosing, even unconsciously, to think about a problem at work or a customer's needs. This is discretionary effort, effort that cannot be forced, measured, or required. It only occurs when employees genuinely care about the success of the organization.

Innovation thrives in an environment of high trust, social capital. Most innovations are not the product of one person thinking alone. Rather they are the result of thinking together, sharing ideas, brainstorming and allowing your idea to be criticized by your associates. High trust cultures are high innovation cultures. If you examine low trust cultures, such as in the Middle East, you will find very low rates of innovation. Companies in which there is a culture of fear, rather than a culture that celebrates successes, will have low rates of innovation.

The degree of competence and continual education of employees, lays the foundation for high innovation. When an individual is continually seeking the latest knowledge, the latest experiments, the latest inventions or theories, his or her mind is playing in the intellectual waters in which innovations float to the top.

The success of Honda and Toyota over U.S. automobile companies was the result of their fanatic dedication to process and product innovation. The success of Wal-Mart, Home Depot, L. L. Bean or McDonald's is all about process innovation in their industries. Processes either create or minimize cost. They assure either consistency and reliability or the unfortunate alternative. Like other forms of capital, the quality of the work process and technological innovations that create an advantage for customers is a significant asset.

Innovations may be one of four types or a combination of types: They may be innovations in a product delivered to customers, or they may be innovations in process, how they are delivered or produced. Either product or process innovations may be small incremental improvements; or they may be large game changing breakthroughs. The way each of these is encouraged is different.

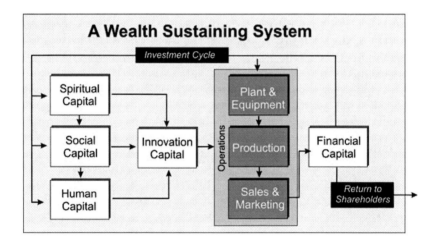

FINANCIAL CAPITAL:

Financial capital is the tradition understanding of capital assets. It may be measured as balance sheet assets or as the value of present and projected cash flows.

For generations, students of economics will be studying the economic crisis of this time, and there will be endless theories and debates about its cause. Most of those theories and debates will focus on interest rates, the Federal Reserve policies, government spending and taxation, and the degree of risks or leverage held by both individuals and institutions. In other words, most will focus on how money caused the disappearance of money. Most will not understand the relationship between the spiritual, social, human and innovation antecedents that precipitated the decline.

Lehman, Bear Sterns and AIG did not collapse because of the lack of money. On the contrary, they had access to most of the wealth of the world. What they lost was not money. They lost the antecedents to money. They lost a system of values and purpose that had created trust with their clients. It then required only minor triggering events to cause a rapid loss of trust in the market place. This loss of trust then caused the immediate outflow of capital. It was the failure of spiritual, social and human capital that caused the collapse of these institutions.

RESPONDING TO THE STRATEGIC LANDSCAPE:

Developing an internal strategy requires an understanding of the environment, the landscape on which you must compete.

All living organisms survive by adapting to their environment. All systems that survive are "open-systems," which simply means that they are open to influence, to feedback and change from their

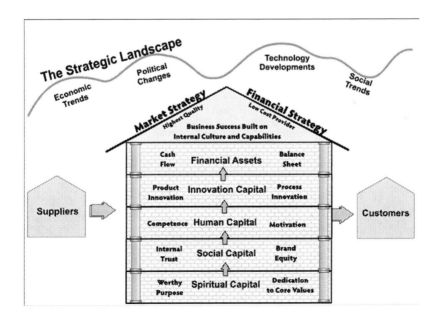

environments. The strategic house of every corporation sits on a landscape and that landscape is constantly changing. Modern organizations have no choice but to change, to adapt themselves in response to the landscape around them.

There are six elements to the landscape of every organization. First are the customers and suppliers who create requirements and who must meet your requirements. Second are the external changes in economic trends, political changes, technology developments and social trends. How do these create a demand for adaptation? The following are quick and simple examples. Every organization operates on a different landscape and it is the job of strategic managers to know their landscape and how they need to respond.

SUPPLIERS:

Lean organization does not operate within one house. It operates in a long series of houses, each adapting to the needs of the other. When Japanese manufacturers moved operations to the United States one of their greatest concerns was the ability to establish a supplier community that could provide the high quality, just-in-time, input required for their operations. They have invested a great deal of resources training and consulting with these suppliers. This attention to the operations of suppliers, many of whom also supplied GM, Ford and Chrysler, had a profound impact on the landscape of the entire industry.

CUSTOMERS:

Customers are the most important part of the landscape for any business. Customer expectations and preferences change daily and they almost always change in the direction of tighter demands, lower cost, and more responsive supply delivery. Listening, sensing, and adapting to the needs of customers is one of the most important capabilities for any business.

ECONOMIC TRENDS:

For about ten years I consulted with several major oil companies. During that time they were constantly engaged in scenario planning, attempting to predict the future price of crude oil. The price of crude oil is directly related to global economic activity. The price of crude determines the economic viability of exploration and production activity. In order to justify the costs of exploratory drilling and then production at a deep-water site in the Gulf of Mexico oil prices must be above a certain level. Whether to build additional refinery capacity, hire explorationists, invest in property leases, or further exploit existing wells all is determined by the expected future price of crude oil. The need for internal strategic capabilities (the number of explorationists employed, for example) will determine the ability to meet strategic goals. Every industry has similar relationships with economic activity. Both internal and external strategy (market and financial) are dependent on these economic trends.

POLITICAL CHANGES:

As I write this the number one focus of congress is on the health care debate, the role the government will play, and the costs associate with any revision of our health care system. This political debate not only affects every company in the health care industry, but every company that currently buys, or may in the future buy, health insurance for its employees. While this will have a huge impact on business in the United States, it is only one of hundreds of ways that political decisions impact corporations. Sensing and responding intelligently to changes in law is critical to the strategy of every company.

TECHNOLOGY DEVELOPMENTS:

It is a rare company that is not required to adapt to changes in technology, changes that will be adopted by competitors. Whether it is robots in a factory, CRM software, or new software for decision making or knowledge management, virtually every company lives on a landscape of competitive technologies.

SOCIAL TRENDS:

Are you marketing to Latinos? Is your workplace friendly to working mothers? Social trends affect both internal and external relationships. A lack of sensitivity to social changes can lead to big trouble and the loss of social capital. One of the largest law firms in Atlanta a few years ago had an employee outing at Lake Lanier. As part of the "fun" to welcome new associates they encouraged all the new woman associates to engage in a wet t-shirt contest. This is a law firm that litigates sexual harassment and every other possible offense. What were they thinking! Of course one of their own associates sued them. It is easy to become conditioned to the habits of the old culture and be blinded to social trends... even when your brain should know otherwise.

CHAPTER 3

A PROCESS FOR DESIGNING
STRUCTURE, SYSTEMS AND SYMBOLS

Now that you know what must be changed to instill lean culture you now need a process, an action plan to move forward. This chapter will outline a process for aligning structure, systems and symbols. The second part of this book is an action plan for implementing the daily habits, the skills and style, of lean culture.

The following four D's (*Discover, Dream, Design,* and *Develop*) provide a proven road map. There will generally be a "design team" chartered to design the future organization and culture. It may follow these four stages of work.

STAGE 1: DISCOVER

To discover is to learn. Before you can design the future you must have ideas, alternatives, benchmarks that can guide you in your decisions. Discovery leads to the dream of a better future.

Many different activities can be employed during the discovery phase, but you can generally divide them into *external* and *internal* discovery.

External discovery will include benchmarking industry leaders and those who may have developed excellent cultures. Your change management team, or leadership team, should survey customers and suppliers to identify those who might be willing to share their best practices. Internal discovery involves the search for best practices within.

Many improvement efforts have begun with a search for the guilty, to be followed by a good hanging, and a sigh of relief. In short order, it will be time to search again. Nothing systemic has changed. Most change efforts over the past few decades have been problem centered. The nature of change efforts both reflect the current culture, and have an impact on the subsequent culture. It is certainly desirable that a change process reflects the type of culture it is seeking to create. The way by which one goes about creating change, even at the outset of the process, will create and reinforce expectations. A search for the guilty obviously increases fear and reduces participation in that improvement. A positive approach does the opposite.

In the last few years, a new approach to change has emerged called *Appreciative Inquiry.*

Appreciative inquiry is "the study and exploration of what gives life to human systems when they function at their best. This approach to personal change and organization change is based on the assumption that questions and dialogue about strengths, successes, values, hopes and dreams are transformational." [3]

Market Strategy — Highest Quality

Financial Strategy — Low Cost Provider

Business Success Built on Internal Culture and Capabilities

Structure | Systems | Skills | Style | Symbols

Discover — Dream — Design — Develop

The "How" of Building the Culture:
The 4D's are the Process of Analysis and Change

Just as the field of positive psychology has argued that more may be gained by studying those who are mentally and emotionally healthy, appreciative inquiry focuses on strengths and positive characteristics within the organization.

---

[3] Whitney, Diana & Trosten-Bloom, Amanda. *The Power of Appreciative Inquiry: A Practical Guide to Positive Change.* San Francisco, Barrett-Koehler Publishers, Inc. 2003.

Some years ago, I participated in the development of a program for Met Life called Achieving Personal Quality. This series of videos and workbooks focused on effective models, examples of personal quality within Met Life. They videotaped interviews of individual Met Life employees who were examples of excellence. The individuals represented many different functions and levels in the organization. I remember watching the video of a carpenter who worked in the maintenance area of the Met Life building. He spoke with great passion about his apprenticeship as a young boy in Italy with a cabinetmaker. With great emphasis, he distinguished between a "cabinet maker" and a carpenter. He emphasized the skill and attention to detail of a cabinetmaker, and one could tell by watching this interview how this cabinetmaker had instilled in his young apprentice the pride of workmanship. Met Life was not trying to train cabinetmakers. But observing and understanding this positive model, and discussing, meditating on the personal qualities of this individual and how those qualities might be important in your own life, was a powerful learning experience. Although at the time no one had ever used the term appreciative inquiry, this was an example of it. The inquiry focused on the personal performance of an effective individual, his qualities, and how these were achieved.

Appreciative inquiry begins with choosing an "affirmative topic," one that lends itself to an exploration of positive qualities. The Met Life program of Achieving Personal Quality began with an inquiry into "what does personal excellence or personal quality look like at Met Life?"

I studied the dozen most successful salesmen selling Mack Trucks and asked the question "to what characteristics or behavior do the best salesmen attribute their success." We interviewed and videotaped these salesmen and presented a summary of *The Habits of Highly Successful Sales Professionals* at Mack Trucks as a video to all eight hundred salesmen and women. This served to reinforce those qualities in the sales force as a group.

Each of the two words, Appreciation and Inquiry, has important meaning. We have already discussed the power of appreciation, and the ways in which it can effectively change both personal habits and a culture. The word inquiry is important because it implies that the change agents, whether external consultants or internal change agents, are not presenting themselves as those who know the answers. Rather, it implies that through the process of asking questions, of shared discovery, all participants will learn and all will benefit. The internal environment begins with clarification of the guiding values, mission, vision and strategy. These principles and ideas should give direction to all of the work of the design process. It is the responsibility of the steering team to provide this guidance.

Three different types of discovery activities may be used: individual interviews, small focus groups, or large scale conferences. The design team members may develop a series of interview questions focusing first on the strengths and positive performance of the organization and then on wishes, desires, or needs. They may split up into pairs to go interview customers and suppliers, or they may schedule focus groups. I have seen customers speak to conferences of more than a hundred employees at Corning and other companies to give their views on what the company does well and what they would like to see in the future.

DISCOVERING THE PROCESS

The next step is mapping the core work process. The design team may spend a good bit of time developing this graphic depiction of the work of the organization. As they discover this map they will want to ask questions about the organizations strengths and discover stories about how individuals or teams have done heroic things to serve their customers and improve the product or service. These stories will be important in developing the dream of the future organization.

The design team will also want to discover the true nature of the flow of the core work process, from incoming materials and information, to the output of products, services or information. Their map should identify the value stream, the net value of the process minus the time and costs in things and people. To the degree possible, each step should be identified that adds value as well as steps that are of questionable value. They should also discover where quality problems occur through the process. The chapter on process mapping will provide more details.

The design team will then want to identify all of the enabling processes, those that support and make the core process successful. Depending on the scope of their effort, they may want to map these processes and follow the same steps they did for the core process.

STAGE 2: DREAM

To dream is to imagine a better future. To dream is to image what could be versus what is. To say that you should "dream" in the context of business may sound foolish. But all significant change is based on a dream of a significantly better future.

There are three BIG questions that can help members of the organization develop dreams about their future:

- Considering our mission as an organization, what would be the ideal future service or product for our customers? What would this look like? How would it make our customers feel?
- What would make this organization the world's best place to work while we accomplish our mission? What would it feel like? What about the work setting would provide the most encouragement and development for the members of our organization?
- How would the first two questions make us a great business, and help us achieve great business results?

You may at first think "What do these questions have to do with becoming a lean organization?" Becoming lean means doing those things that most serve your customer's needs and eliminating those things that add no value to your customer. Toyota did not develop the Prius by simply focusing on eliminating waste. Apple did not develop the iPad by mapping processes to eliminating waste. They developed the iPad by dreaming about the future. They imagined the ideal device to carry around so that you could browse the web, read email and read books. By doing this they deployed resources toward those activities that they imagined would add the most value to their customers.

Around each of these three big questions it will not be hard to image many other questions. There are numerous exercises and fun ways to explore the dream. For example you can ask individuals or small groups to write an article for the Wall Street Journal that is doing a story on your company ten years from now. The WSJ is writing an article about your company as a success story that will inspires others. The story should reflect everything you want the company to be. What you will be able to say about the company? You can also call upon the creative imagination of members of your organization by asking them to develop and act out skits that reflect the dream of your future company. These skits, for example, could be at a cocktail party. The President of the United States, ten years from now, is having a dinner and cocktail party for winners of the National Quality Award. As a member of the team who helped make this happen, you have been invited. Now write a script and act out the conversation where you are explaining to others at the cocktail party what you did that made your company worthy to win this award.

These are just examples of some of the things you can do to encourage the development of the dream. Remember that people dream in groups. In other words, one person's story stimulates ideas in another. Have you ever watched a group sitting around and imagining what could happen together? They feed on each other, laugh with each other, and from the dialogue comes a collective dream that none of them alone would have imagined.

Out of the discovery and dream stage it will be desirable to form a "consensus dream." Some elements of this may become clear in large group meetings, but it will probably take more clear form in meetings by the smaller design team. Out of all the dreams, some of which may be out in left field, you now need to develop a dream that becomes the real target.

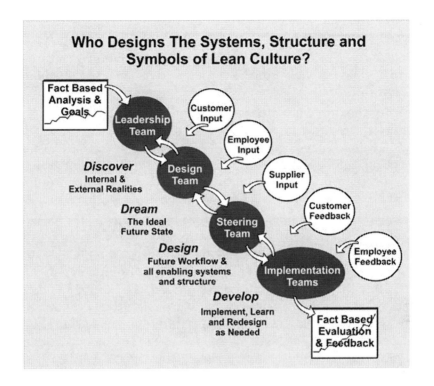

STAGE 3: DESIGN

Based on the discovery and the dream, it is now time to begin the design process. While the dream phase put practical concerns and all forms of skepticism aside; now is the time to begin to get practical. Now is the time to say, "Ok, what can we actually do that will make that dream come true?"

During the Discovery and Dream process you have generated a long list of things you would like to change. Now you have to organize those and start designing in some logical manner. The beginning point should be the core work process. It is best if you start with a clean sheet of paper and ask the question "if we were starting a new company and had no restraint, what would we design to be the ideal process?"

The organization exists for the purpose of creating the output of the core work process. The enabling processes (human resources, information systems, etc.) should be designed to support and optimize the core work process. At this stage the design team may either redesign those processes (they may not have the right people on the design team and it may not be within their charter); or, they may create process requirements for the enabling processes.

Once the core work process is designed the design team begins to address the structure and systems around the process. There is one BIG rule as they begin to do this. Design the organization from the bottom up! In other words, what is the organization of groups at the first level, where the work is done, that will maximize the probability that the work will be done in the best possible way.

This is the beginning of structure. The structure of society begins with the structure of the family. The beginning of organization structure should be the design of the small work groups who will manage and improve their work on a day-to-day basis. After the first level groups are formed, the question is then asked "What help do they need to do their work in the best possible way?" Think about how this question is different than asking "How many managers are needed?" If you ask what help is needed you will get a very different answer, and it will be a more "lean" answer. If the right training, information, tools, decision authority, and coaching are provided to the team, you will find that far less management is needed.

Similar questions are then asked about all of the systems in the organization. For example:

- How can the information systems most help those who do the work?
- What method of presentation and delivery of information would be most helpful to the teams?
- What training systems would most enable teams and individuals to do their job in the ideal way?
- What methods and patterns of communication would be most helpful and encouraging to employees?

The design team will identify all of the relevant systems that support the core work, and will then develop a list of questions and issues to be addressed in their design work.

STAGE 4: DEVELOP:

Rather than think of any design as complete, or finished, it is best to acknowledge the inevitable reality that you have only done your best at this time. As groups set about implementing the new design, they will quickly find ways to improve it. Rather than create any resistance to this, it is best to plan for it, encourage it and hope that the process of implementation is one of on-going development and learning.

Having observed more than one hundred organization design projects roughly following this model, it has always surprised me that an enormous amount of energy is put into the process of design, and then there is a letdown when it comes to implementation. The value of the design can be lost if similar energy is not invested in the implementation itself. The implementation must be managed. Good project management skills now need to be used.

It is important that everyone involved has an attitude of continuous improvement when implementing the new systems or structure. It will never be 100% right! It will be your best shot at this point in time. However, once you start implementing the new design you will start learning. You will find that some of the pieces don't fit together perfectly, or you may find you have not thought of some element of the process that also needs to be aligned with the new process you have designed. If you view these discoveries as failures, you will stifle the learning process. It is much better to understand that these are the natural process of learning that occurs during implementation.

CHAPTER *4*

MANAGING IMPLEMENTATION

It is often easy to identify what you want to accomplish. Accomplishing it is much more difficult. The hard part is developing and sticking to a plan that will get you there. This is change management.

Most difficulties in managing change in an organization do not arise because people are trying to change the wrong things or accomplish the wrong goals. Rather, the difficulties arise from failures in the process of getting there.

PRINCIPLES OF CHANGE MANAGEMENT

The following *principles* have proven to lead to successful implementation.

UNITED WE SUCCEED!

The principle of unity is one of the first principles of any group performance. It is recognized by every general of every army. It is recognized by every coach of every sports team. It applies to families, communities, countries, companies and work teams.

The progress of the human race can be seen as the progress of increasing circles of unity from the family to tribe, to city state and religion, to nations and global alliances and global culture.

Civilizations are described in a process of growth as achieving *integration* and when in decline they are in *disintegration*.

Why do we say "she has her act together?" "Wow is he coming unglued." In our popular culture we intuitively recognize the value of connections versus fragmentation, integration versus disintegration. Unity within self, unity of groups, unity of companies or countries, results in superior performance.

So, what are the implications of this principle when building a lean culture? Do it all together; top to bottom in the organization. The worst mistake in managing change is to say, "Well, those folks need it more than anyone else, so let's start there." That will guarantee failure. "Those folks" will resist like the devil because they will resent being singled out as the problem group.

HIGH INVOLVEMENT EQUALS HIGH COMMITMENT

Why is democracy a better form of government than autocracies? Democracy is messy, noisy, confusing and troublesome in so many ways. It's expensive, too. Why not the clean clear command of authority instead? We all know the answer intuitively. We know that there is a collective intelligence, a collective mind, or "the wisdom of the people" that Thomas Jefferson recognized.

High involvement in the work place creates collective intelligence. The mere act of being asked a question increases mental exercise that builds connections that we call intelligence. When an employee looks at a graph of her team's performance, and asks "why," the brain cells go to work. A learning organization is an organization comprised of individual members who are constantly prompted to ask "why?" The team process is simply a way to stimulate thinking and learning among every member of the organization.

The most successful change processes are those in which the managers and employees, the real owners of the workplace, are fully engaged in analyzing, brainstorming and deciding about the change process. You implement what you own! If you own the creation of the solution, you will implement that solution.

BE BUSINESS FOCUSED

Stephen Covey said "begin with the end in mind." Good advice. If you want to achieve improvements in business performance, start with a focus on business performance.

Over the last twenty years there have been numerous change processes all of which have contributed some useful concept. However, after periods of enthusiasm and apparent success, they have faded in popularity to be replaced by a new wave of enthusiasm claiming to be the solution to management ills. When enthusiasm in employee involvement, Total Quality Management, or reengineering declined it was due to the business failure of companies that had been held up as models. Florida Power & Light and the Wallace Company both won the United States National Quality Award and immediately encountered severe business failure. Motorola, the founding home of the Six Sigma quality management process, was in business decline during most of their focus on Six Sigma. That does not mean that there is anything wrong with Six Sigma, it simply means that successful Six Sigma projects do not necessarily equate to improved business performance.

Analysis of many change failures leads back to the same point. Begin with the end in mind. What results do you really want to achieve? If you want to achieve improvement in business performance you are well advised to design that connection into the change process from the beginning. The very idea of moving toward a "business team" approach is that every team and every employee is clearly focused on measurable business results they can impact.

GET OUT OF YOUR VILLAGE

Several times I have been hired to assist companies when I have had no prior experience in their industry. Twice I remember telling the executive who was hiring me that I had no experience in his industry and was told that was good. They wanted someone who was not part of the industry culture, someone who could see beyond the walls of how things are normally done within that industry.

Chinese villagers given the mandate to design the "ideal" house and assured that they have total freedom to design without any restrictions, and with an unlimited budget, will not design a Williamsburg Colonial or a "Frank Lloyd Wright" contemporary home. They only have Chinese village maps imprinted in their minds. They might design the best house to ever come out of their village, but it would look a lot like previous village houses. We are all Chinese villagers! Do the same exercise in an American mid-west village and they will not design a Chinese looking home. They have no map to follow that would get them there.

If you ask those who work in a traditional restaurant, a bank, a hospital, or manufacturing plant, to design the ideal work flow, the ideal process or organization and management, their natural tendency will be to design a slightly improved version of their own organization. They are following their own "Chinese Village" maps. On the other hand, if you take those who work in a hospital and have them study the process of serving fast food in a McDonald's restaurant and now have them design "McHospital" you may experience a significant breakthrough. It is important to go through exercises like this, not on the assumption that "McHospital" will be the right answer, but rather because it encourages the participants to think out-of-the-box.

MAKE IT MATTER — REINFORCE IMPROVEMENT

We do what matters. It is the job of leadership to make important things matter. Business performance, customer satisfaction, innovation, and eliminating waste, are among the things that matter to the organization.

Many improvement efforts fail for the very simple reason that managers fail to make it matter. When you implement the team structure in the organization there should be a regular review and accountability process. Monthly and/or quarterly reviews by higher level teams are an important way to provide motivation for improvement. Once teams are established, they will create a balanced scorecard and map their processes. This should be shared with teams above and perhaps those below. Goals should be established for improvement and teams should then report back what they have done. This sharing is both a motivation process and a learning process. You will learn from what other teams are doing to improve. Those lessons should be shared across the team structure.

THE PSYCHOLOGY OF A CHANGE PROCESS

Leadership is an essential component of any change process. Why? Because changing the culture of an organization is not a mechanical process. It requires the right psychology, motivation and human effort. Leaders need to promote, encourage, reinforce and model the change in order to create the psychology needed.

Almost every change process transitions through some predictable psychological stages.

Romance Stage: When the relationship begins the change effort is sold on a dream, the dream of a better way, an easier life, a more fulfilling work place, and to achieve better business results that will provide security and opportunities for all. This creates a good deal of enthusiasm, but of course no one has done any work yet. No sacrifices have been made to raise any questions about the cost-benefit of the effort. And, of course, there are no results yet.

Pregnancy and Labor: Now things begin to get hard. Now is when encouragement and leadership is most needed. The seed is planted and the work of growth has begun, stretching our capacity, requiring sacrifices to be made, extra effort, and discipline. Somehow, the romance begins to fade. There still aren't any results

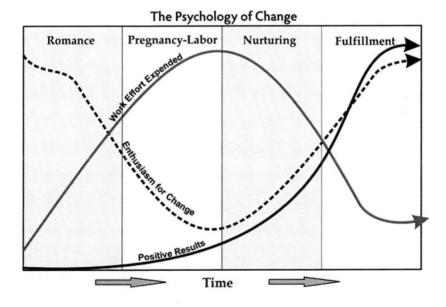

The Psychology of Change

to prove the value of the effort, and as the work and sacrifice increase the enthusiasm drops. In the last stage of labor it is normal to see one party snapping at the other, saying something like "how could you do this to me?!! Whose dumb idea was this?"

Nurturing: A point comes when the effort begins to bear fruit and the infant emerges smiling, screaming, and pooping. With basic patterns of behavior and skills established, the effort is not so difficult anymore. There is an acceptance of the process and the first signs of actual results begin to appear. There is still the need for coaching, training, encouragement and discipline. But, it begins to be less difficult and the early results begin to renew some enthusiasm.

Fulfillment: The group begins to achieve *mastery*, the skill and knowledge to perform are now established and a *flow* begins to be achieved. Results are now increasing in frequency and a critical mass of employees is experiencing these results. A tipping point is now achieved when enthusiasm increases, the effort is much less, and the results are proving the value of the effort. Now most people admit that this was they actually are the parents of this idea, after all. But, like all good things, it will still require effort and discipline to maintain.

ACTION LEARNING: DOING, DELIVERABLES AND ACCOUNTABILITY

A great deal of the training conducted by our organizations is not effective. There are two reasons for this: first most training is conducted in large blocks of several days for the convenience of trainers. Unfortunately, this is not how we learn best. Second, most training does not require application. Third, there is rarely accountability for doing things differently following training.

The process of Lean Team Management is designed to correct for each of these common failures. The training component of LTM is conducted in weekly, bi-weekly or monthly training sessions in the natural teams. They deal with their issues, their performance, and their customers. Each team is assigned a coach who both delivers the training and provides feedback to the team leader and the team. The coaches work as a team to share experiences and support one another. The best use of an external consultant is to support these internal coaches. Finally, a process of accountability is established so that teams and their leaders are recognized for their progress and held accountable for non-performance.

Lean Team Management is not simply about learning. It is about doing and performing. It is about implementing a new way of managing the organization. This workbook and associated training and coaching are designed to elicit new behavior on the part of managers and teams.

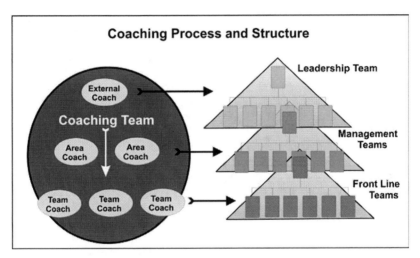

It is important that you manage the process of implementation. That means that there should be clear expectations in terms of what each team will do to implement LTM. The following is a list of "deliverables," things that a team will do to demonstrate their learning and to improve their functioning as a team. The deliverables correspond to training modules or chapters in the LTM manual.

It will be helpful if the coach tracks the training modules completed and the deliverables completed for each team. This can be done on an Excel spreadsheet. This will help motivate the team and keep them on track in their development.

The following twenty-five items are auditable deliverables that are completed as a team progresses through their training. These action items are the implementation of the LTM process for any given team. The related chapters are those in the LTM workbook.

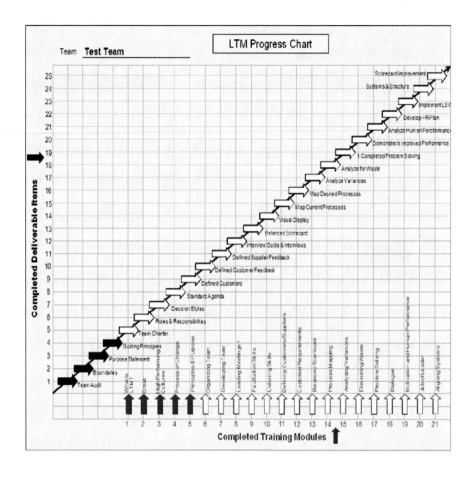

Key Deliverable to be Completed by Each Team	Related Chapter In LTM Manual
1. The team has evaluated its own performance and gaps to become a high performing team.	Introduction and Appendix
2. The team has developed an initial definition of the process or processes for which it is responsible and the boundaries of those processes (SIPOC).	Chapter 3
3. The team has a defined a statement of purpose or mission.	Chapter 3
4. The team has reached consensus on a code of conduct or principles by which it will live and agreed on how it will hold it's self-accountable.	Chapter 3
5. The team has defined its charter and asked its leader or manager to confirm or modify that charter.	Chapter 3
6. The team has defined roles and responsibilities within the team.	Chapter 4
7. The team has agreed which decisions will be command, consultative, or consensus decisions.	Chapter 6
8. The team has developed and agreed on a standard agenda.	Chapter 7
9. The team has defined its customers and suppliers.	Chapter 11
10. The team has defined how it will receive periodic feedback from its customers.	Chapter 11

11. The team has agreed on a periodic process for providing feedback to its suppliers.	Chapter 11
12. The team has developed a guide or agreed on how it will interview its customers, and has conducted those interviews and evaluated the results.	Chapter 12
13. The team has developed a balanced scorecard with process, customer satisfaction, financial and development measures.	Chapter 13
14. The team has posted graphs that are visual and up-to-date that reflects performance of the measures on its scorecard.	Chapter 13
15. The team has mapped one current state process and found improvements in that process.	Chapter 14
16. The team has mapped the "ideal" or desired process for its key processes.	Chapter 14
17. The team has analyzed variation and identified causes of variation for its key performance measures.	Chapter 15
18. The team has analyzed its process to find waste, using the seven forms of waste as a guide.	Chapter 16
19. The team has studied the problem-solving model and taken one problem completely through the problem-solving process.	Chapter 17

20. Team has implemented and demonstrated improvement in one of the measures using the problem-solving model.	Chapter 17
21. The team has analyzed a human performance issue and developed a plan for improving that performance.	Chapter 18
22. The team has agreed on, and implemented a plan to reinforce desired performance.	Chapter 18
23. The team has agreed on the work of leaders and implemented a plan of leader standard work.	Chapter 21
24. The team has identified systems that can be modified to assist them in their efforts to improve performance.	Chapter 19
25. The key measures of performance are currently trending up, or are within ten percent of peak performance in the past year.	All Chapters

PART TWO

TACTICS – BE THE CHANGE!
DEVELOPING THE DAILY HABITS OF LEAN CULTURE

CHAPTER 5

THE WORK OF TEAMS – MANAGING THE CORE WORK

Lean organizations are a social system, a culture, as well as a technical system. At the heart of that social system is the small work group both at the front line level and at all levels of management. It doesn't matter whether your organization is entirely comprised of knowledge workers sitting at desks, service providers in a not-for-profit organization, or assembly line workers in a manufacturing plant; the most effective organizations are all built on the foundation of effective teams. And, they start at the top.

"What are the truly important organizational features of a lean plant - the specific aspects of plant operations that account for up to half of the overall performance differences among plants across the world? The truly lean plant has two key organizational features: It transfers the maximum number of tasks and responsibilities to those workers actually adding value to the car on the line, and it has in place a system for detecting defects that quickly traces every problem, once discovered, to its ultimate cause....So in the end, *it is the dynamic work team that emerges as the heart of the lean factory.*"[4]

---

[4] Womack, J.P., Jones, D. T., and Roos D. *The Machine That Changed the World.* New York: Rawson Associates, 1990, P. 99.

The majority of companies implementing lean organization are not achieving the results they could achieve because they are primarily focused on the technical things, the JIT, Kanban, etc. All of the technical arrangements of work and materials amount to no more than half of what creates the genuine competitive advantage of lean. The other half is the human side, the culture of the organization. This is the hard part because it is about you – how you think, feel and behave. It is about the relationships between team members, between different functions and levels in the organization. It is about trust. This is the hard part.

Lean Team Management (LTM) is the implementation of continuous improvement through every team, at every level of the organization. It is turning the daily management process into a process of continuous improvement. It is a way to implement lean culture in a systematic way through the "normal" decision-making structure of the organization.

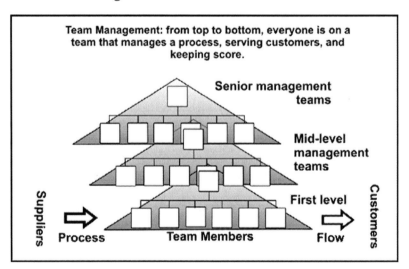

The intention of LTM is to combine every proven and useful practice to create an organization in which every team is business focused and every individual feels that he or she is contributing to business performance. This unity of purpose enhances the dignity of every individual in the organization.

HIGH PERFORMING TEAMS = HIGH PERFORMING CULTURE

The family is the first learning organization where values are formed and work habits are learned. Similarly, the small group structure, the team, is the foundation of successful organization. The degree to which teams are structured, trained, and encouraged to take responsibility for performance and continuous improvement is the degree to which the organization will perform at a high level.

A word about language: Many different terms have been used to describe small work groups. The term "self-managing teams" was popular for a time. However, no team is truly self-managing. Everyone, including the CEO of the company, has a manager. In manufacturing the term "work cell" is often used to describe a small work area and the group that completes a discrete work product. But, that term doesn't say anything about the human dynamics of the group. In this writer's opinion, the most appropriate term is "high performing team."

It is important to note that this term applies equally to first level work teams and teams that manage a large organization. If the team that leads an organization is not a high performing team, it will make little difference whether or not the teams on the first level are high performing.

What defines a group of people as a high performance team?

You are a high performance team if...

- *...You have on-going responsibility for a work process that results in business revenue, examines operating costs or meets customer satisfaction requirements.*
- *...you know your customers and communicate with those customers concerning their requirements and satisfaction.*
- *...you have a balanced scorecard that includes process, finance, customer satisfaction and learning or development measures*
- *...you measure your operating process performance in terms of quality and productivity.*

- *...you have the capability and responsibility to evaluate your performance, solve problems and make decisions to continuously improve your operations.*
- *...your team has demonstrated competence in each of the above tasks.*

LEADERSHIP TEAMS

Just as every associate doing front line work should be a member of a team, every manager should also be a member of a team. If you think about it, the Board of Directors of a company is a team. The CEO and his senior business unit leaders are, or should be, a team.

Leadership teams also have responsibility for processes. For example, if you are the CEO of a pharmaceutical company, your team is probably comprised of the VPs of R&D, Sales and Marketing, and Manufacturing. Also on your team are the senior staff positions for Finance, Legal, Human Resources, etc. This team shares responsibility for the process by which the company achieves its major financial strategy. It is also responsible for the creation of brand equity, social capital in the market place. It is also responsible for the culture of the organization. These are processes, or the result of processes, that cannot be controlled by any one executive. The VP of Finance does not actually control the finances of the organization. Finances are controlled by the success of the research labs, the sales and marketing process, and others. To succeed it is essential that this team work together, solving problems and developing plans together. This team is responsible for strategy and no member, including the CEO can control strategy on his or her own. It requires the whole team.

Too often executives and managers see themselves as "Lone Rangers" riding through the organization to find the bad guys and solve problems on their own. This is largely a management myth. Many research studies have demonstrated that successful leaders are those who are successful at building a strong team around them, working well with that team, and giving credit to the team. In other words, they are good team leaders.

One of the best qualities of a leader is humility. Contrary to the image of the charismatic leader, most corporate executives who achieve sustained superior performance are not the demanding cheerleader. Rather, they are patient, and behave with humility. Jim Collins, in *Good To Great*[5] documents leaders who possess this quality of humility. He describes what he calls Level 5 Leadership: *"We were surprised, shocked really, to discover the type of leadership required for turning a good company into a great one. Compared to high-profile leaders with big personalities who make head-lines and become celebrities, the good-to-great leaders seem to have come from Mars. Self-effacing, quiet, reserved, even shy – these leaders are a paradoxical blend of personal humility and professional will. They are more like Lincoln and Socrates than Patton or Caesar."* [6]

Humility is being open to the ideas of others. Humility is the ability to learn and change course when the evidence points in a different direction. Humility is the capacity to suspend judgment and listen to the voices of others. It is this kind of leadership that is most successful on leadership teams and in lean organizations.

TYPES OF TEAMS

Teams can be organized in more than one way, for more than one purpose. It is important to be clear which kind of team you are organizing. A team may be an on-going process management team, a project improvement team formed under Six Sigma or TQM, a knowledge management team, or a leadership team.

LEAN PROCESS MANAGEMENT TEAMS

These may also be called work teams, work cells, front line teams, or simply the teams in the organization that do the core work. Most organizations are a chain of process management teams that follow the flow of the process from input to output. Most of the associates working in most organizations will be members of these teams. Lean organizations have organized all front line employees into teams who take ownership of their work process.

---

[5] Collins, Jim. *Good to Great.* Harper Business, New York: 2001

[6] Ibid. pp. 12-13.

The basic idea of *Lean Team Management* is that all levels of the organization are formed into permanent teams that engage in continuous improvement of their work. These teams are linked together, with each team defining and getting feedback from its customers and management levels providing coordination and leadership to the teams. The goals, scorecards, and work of these teams are all linked together to create a unity of energy and effort.

Process management teams may be a work cell, composed of associates who work within a very close physical area, often rotating jobs, and learning each other's skills so they can pitch in and smooth the flow of work.

PROJECT IMPROVEMENT TEAMS

Process management teams can only improve the process within their boundaries. In almost every organization there are problems that cut across teams. For example, there may be issues of the environment (temperature, air quality, etc.) that are not owned by any one team. There may also be methodologies or equipment that are used by more than one team. No one team will have the scope of authority to decide to change these issues. These require a project improvement team.

Project improvement teams are temporary. They are not the primary job of any member, but members who work on different teams will serve on a project team to find a solution to a particular problem.

Project teams may be chosen to work on a problem by the management team, or process teams may identify a problem beyond their control and request that a project team be formed to attack that problem.

KNOWLEDGE MANAGEMENT TEAMS

Most organizations have teams that are organized around a knowledge area. Engineers, quality professionals, or other professional groups may serve on two different teams at the same time. They may serve on a team of subject matter experts, those with a similar expertise or knowledge base. They may also serve on a management or project team that is responsible for the horizontal flow from suppliers to customers.

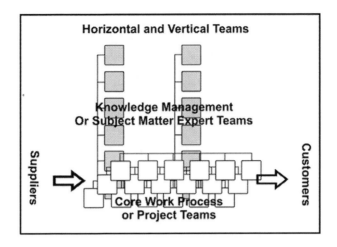

In a petroleum exploration and production organization, teams were formed both to support the exploration and production work process and to support the development of professional competencies and methods. Civil and structural engineers, geologists, economists, and other experts each had a "home room," a team that served their needs for professional development. However, the real work was done on project teams assigned to develop an "asset", a property that contained oil reserves. The project team might work for several years on the development of that asset. A geologist or economist might be the only one with his or her expertise serving on that team. Without the "home room" of the expert team they would soon become lost in the organization.

CHAPTER 6

ORGANIZING TEAMS

The purpose of any organization's structure should be to optimize the flow of the core work that serves the needs of customers. Too often the structure inhibits the flow of the work. The design of organization structure, and all the systems that enable the flow of work, should begin at the first level of the organization. Never design the structure from the top down. Always design the structure from the bottom up.

The structure should follow the flow of the work process, with teams formed to continuously improve and control each set of operations. Optimize the capability of the team by asking what information, skills, tools, and help they need. Design these into the formation of the team. Toss out all previous management titles and assumptions. Then ask, what help does the team need from others? The answer to this question will define the functions of the first level of management. Then ask what human qualities are needed to best fulfill these functions? Then group these team leaders into teams and follow the same process.

This bottom-up, zero-based, organization design usually results in fewer levels.

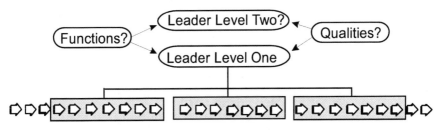

CRITERIA FOR TEAM FORMATION

The following criteria should be considered when defining this structure.

1. **Team Size:** Team size is an important factor in how well they function. How large are families? How large are athletic teams? Groups seem to be able to work well together when they are from five to fifteen members. There is a great deal of research on group decision-making and group dynamics that point to this range as the best size. When groups get larger they become difficult to facilitate. When they are smaller they lack the diversity and dynamics that make for effective decision-making.

2. **Proximity:** Families live within the same physical space. This physical proximity is essential to many of the other dynamics of the family. Similarly, teams function best when the members are situated close enough to rotate jobs, communicate, solve problems, train, and help each other when needed. The use of computer networks and team software are changing this to some degree. However, face-to-face communications is still an important ingredient of group effectiveness.

3. **Control:** Employees want to feel a sense of control. When one feels a lack of control, one feels helpless. Helplessness leads to lost motivation, slow work, and lack of commitment.

4. **Customer Focus:** Teams function best when they have a common focus on the same customer(s). Knowing and satisfying the requirements of *both* internal and external customers is the primary reason for the existence of the organization and ultimately the existence of the team. Teams are best organized to perform as much of the whole process for a customer as possible. Their efforts must be coordinated so they can anticipate and respond to changing customer requirements.

5. **Continuous Learning:** Teams should learn together. People who are mentally healthy, energized, and happy

are people who are in the process of learning and growth. Jobs that are designed with few opportunities for learning are inherently unsatisfying. When designing the responsibilities and composition of a team, one should design the opportunity for continued learning into the structure.

6. **Ability to Solve Problems:** A feeling of empowerment and motivation is derived from participation in problem solving. Employees can solve problems when they have common knowledge, have access to all the pertinent information.

7. **Knowing the Score:** There is no subject in the field of human behavior better researched than the effects of feedback on behavior. It is a simple matter. Cover up the scoreboard at a basketball game, and observe the change in performance. After a short time no one will show up to watch or play. At work, the scoreboard is covered most of the time for most employees.

8. **Shared Work:** When employees work together on the same product or task, they create a feeling of helpfulness which increases self-esteem. A lot of work is organized so employees work alone even though they may be on a team. When all members feel that they are sharing in the effort and output the team will be more successful.

9. **Each Level of the Organization Must Add Value That is Unique.** The first level of teams is responsible for managing the day-to-day work process. Each additional level must be justified by adding specific value to the work of the organization.

OPTIMIZING TEAM CAPABILITY

To optimize the team's capability ask the following questions:

1. What information would optimize the team's performance?
2. What skills, if present within the team, would optimize its performance?

3. What tools or equipment would contribute to performance?
4. What recognition, reward or accountability would enhance the team's performance?
5. What authority to make decisions would enhance their performance?
6. What knowledge and skills are necessary for all team members?
7. What knowledge and skills might be useful to the team if one member of the team were trained as a "Subject Matter Expert" (SME)?

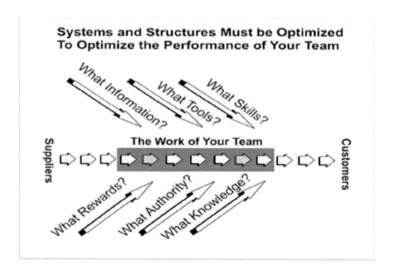

WRITING THE TEAM CHARTER

Whether they are process management teams or project teams, teams should have a written charter that clarifies their boundaries and responsibilities. Every team has boundaries. No team (including the CEO's team) can do "anything" it wants. If teams feel free to take action beyond their area of responsibility, there will soon be chaos in the organization. This charter defines responsibilities and creates a rational linkage between teams.

Developing the team charter should be done when a team is first formed. It should be jointly developed by the team itself and the manager to whom the team is responsible.

The following are the six components that should be in a team charter:

1. Statement of Purpose
2. Process Responsibility
3. Process Boundaries
4. Communication Responsibility
5. Performance Responsibilities
6. Membership and Sponsorship

DEFINING YOUR TEAM'S PURPOSE

Individuals have a personal need to find their purpose and to create their own energy source; they may find it in their faith, family or career. Teams are structured around a common purpose and manage their work to be of service to their customers, those who care about their work. Purpose may be found in genuine caring for others, customers and fellow team members. The purpose of a larger organization should be found in its statement of mission and strategy. Why does the company exist? What will it contribute to the world at large, its customers, shareholders, and employees?

There is a hierarchy of purpose from the eternal to the instant, from the spiritual to the material. We can visualize this as a pyramid. At the top of the pyramid is our largest understanding of our existence. Most of us gain understanding of our purpose from

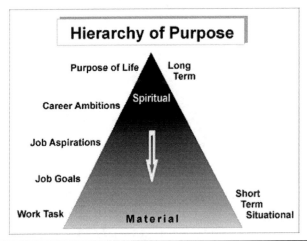

our religion or our parents. The concept of purpose is a spiritual concept. It is not merely intellectual, and it is certainly not material. This is the first subject your team should decide together. Why do you exist, as a team? Who cares about the work you do? How can you have a positive influence on others?

DEFINING OUR CORE WORK PROCESSES

The work of most teams is to manage and improve their work process. The charter should define what processes you "own."

It is important that the team take time at this point to define the basic landscape within which it works. For every team there are inputs and outputs. Someone or some group supplies the team with what it needs to do its work and someone receives its work.

Every team adds value by transforming input to output. It is the team's processes that achieve this transformation. In other words, if your team is a restaurant team, you receive raw food as input. You slice and dice, mix and stir, cook and prepare the food for serving. That is a process that adds value. You serve the food to customers who receive your output and are willing to pay for the value that you have added to the raw input. Almost every team does something similar, although perhaps more complicated than this restaurant team.

This flow, from input to output, is typically described as the team's **SIPOC**: Suppliers, Input, Process, Output, and Customers. In later chapters we will analyze these elements of the system, particularly the work process, in much greater detail. This is the primary focus of continuous improvement efforts. But, for the

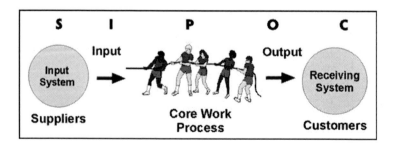

purpose of defining your charter, it will be helpful at this stage to define the basic elements of your SIPOC and particularly the processes for which you are responsible.

COMMUNICATION RESPONSIBILITIES

No team is an island and it has a responsibility to communicate its progress and problems to others. It is important to define to whom the team needs to communicate and how frequently. Managers, customers, suppliers and other teams may need or desire communication from your team. Whom should you keep informed and about what? From whom do you get feedback, and to whom do you give feedback? What information do we need to provide to a manager, and when?

Performance Responsibilities

What are the primary measures of performance for which we are responsible? This should not define specific measures, but the general categories of performance and potential risks of failure.

Later, after we have interviewed our customers, we will create a balanced scorecard that will define how we measure our performance in some detail. But at this stage, for the sake of our Charter, it is useful to define the general types of performance for which we are responsible.

MEMBERSHIP AND SPONSORSHIP

In many cases it is obvious who the team members will be. However, in many organizations there will be teams that include members who are permanently assigned to a different department, but who come together to provide a service or accomplish some other performance. For example in a manufacturing plant there may be a "technical operations" team made up of engineers, chemists and quality experts who work together with line manufacturing employees to manage technical aspects of the work.

Define the members of your team by position or function rather than by name. Over time, the names will change, while the team will continue to fulfill its purpose.

Also define the "sponsor," the position that will approve this charter and authorize the work of the team.

GAINING CHARTER APPROVAL

It is important that the sponsor, whether an individual or a team, review the charter and provide the team with any needed feedback. This "sign-off" will indicate ownership and commitment to the team by the leaders above.

MEMBER ROLES AND RESPONSIBILITIES

A baseball team or a work team succeeds because the players play their position with skill and enthusiasm. Outfielders, pitchers and infielders know their job, their particular contribution to the success of the team. On a team at work there are also distinct and important roles that need to be played.

THE FACILITATOR

Have you ever been in a meeting and sat there wondering just what the topic was and feeling like no one else knew either?

Have you been in a meeting when you felt that everyone was already in agreement, but people just kept talking and no one seemed able to just close the discussion?

Have you been in a meeting where a couple people did all the talking and others were never able to get a word in?

These are just some of the symptoms of poor facilitation that plague meetings. The ability to facilitate a meeting has nothing to do with rank in the organization. I have seen hourly employees on the shop floor do a fantastic job of facilitating a group and I have seen company presidents with virtually no ability to facilitate a meeting. Facilitation is a particular skill that can be learned by anyone, and someone on every team must be a skilled facilitator. Neither formal rank nor formal education guarantees that someone is a good facilitator.

What is facilitation? To facilitate is to make something easy for others. To facilitate a group is to help others in the group make their contribution. Facilitation can be as complicated as planning out an entire series of meetings or it can be the simple act of asking a member of the group if they would like to say something. But most of all, it is the concern for others, the sensitivity to recognize that some are talking so much that others are unable to express their opinions, or the sensitivity to recognize when the group has reached a point of agreement. It is the courage to bring order to what may be the chaos of conversation. It is the most frequent act of leadership that is most needed in organizations today.

And who is the facilitator? There is almost always someone who has the formal role of facilitation in a group. However, and this is extremely important, the actual act of facilitating, of making it easy for others to contribute, is something that every member of the group can and should do. Any member of the group can ask the question "Has everyone had an opportunity to give their opinion?" Or say "It feels like we are in agreement, are we ready to decide?" These are the types of facilitating questions or statements that "move things along" in a group and any member can help make it easy for others or the group to move along.

What is the function of the facilitator? It can be summarized in the following points.

Facilitation is...

- To create a clear agenda and help the group follow the agreed upon agenda.
- To state the topic and help the members of the group stay on the topic.
- To create an environment that is encouraging and safe for all to contribute.
- To help others contribute by inviting or encouraging them in a manner that is helpful to them.
- To be sure contributions are heard by the group.
- To bring topics to a close or decision when the need for dialogue or discussion is complete.
- To restate or clarify decisions in a manner that creates unity of understanding.
- To resolve conflicts that may arise in the group.

THE SCRIBE

There are other formal roles that may be assigned to members of the team. It is very useful to have someone other than the facilitator designated as the "scribe" or secretary of the group. This person will take minutes and distribute those minutes to all of the members of the group. It is helpful if the scribe has a laptop computer and composes the minutes during the meeting. At the end of the meeting he may read the decisions and action steps that were agreed to and check with the group to be sure that he has recorded them correctly. In many organizations the meeting room is connected with wireless Internet access and the scribe can email the minutes to the members of the team before leaving the room.

THE TIMEKEEPER

It is usually assumed that the facilitator or chair of a meeting, who has her eye on the agenda, will take the responsibility of keeping the group on time. However, it is often the case that the facilitator is not a "pure" facilitator, but is an active member of the group, fully engaged in the conversation. In this case, it may be useful to have someone serve as the timekeeper.

SUBJECT MATTER EXPERTS (SME'S)

Many teams have found it helpful to ask a member to specialize in some area of knowledge or some function, that is helpful to the group, but in which it is not necessary for every member to be involved. For example, there may be one person designated as the data management Subject Matter Expert (SME); this could be the member of the team who knows where to get the data for the team's scorecard. He or she will plot that data on graphs and report that data to the team at each team meeting.

Another member of the group may take on the role of helping others with computers and software. In virtually every office there is a computer/software SME, informally recognized as "the person you go to" when you need help with your new computer or software. This person is acting as an SME, even though there may be no formal recognition of this role.

COACH

As teams are developing their skills, it is helpful to have a coach. For the same reasons an athlete benefits from the experience and skill of a coach, a management or work team can also benefit. A coach is not a member of the team. It is very important that the coach not be from within the immediate "power structure" so that he is not hindered by concerns about being "politic" in his feedback to the team. A coach does not go out on the field and play. A coach is on the sidelines and observes the play, and from this perspective can give objective feedback. The coach may meet with the facilitator or leader before a meeting and ask for observations as to the progress and functioning of the team. The coach will then observe and may give the entire team feedback and may also meet with the leader or facilitator to give feedback on how performance of that role can be improved.

It is important that the coach be sensitive to the need to encourage the team, to provide positive feedback on the progress they are making. If the coach only gives feedback on areas in which the team can improve, his advice will soon not be welcomed. It is also important that the coach does not overwhelm the team with thirty things they need to do differently. No one, nor any group, works on thirty things at once. It is great if they work on two or three. Sometime later they can work on the others.

CHAPTER 7

STAGES OF TEAM DEVELOPMENT

In 1965, Bruce Tuckman wrote that there are normal, even necessary stages of development that a team passes through as it matures. These stages, forming, storming, norming and performing, are often presented as if you MUST go through them as you must go through childhood and adolescence. It is true that there is a normal progression in the social development of a team, but there is nothing certain about these stages. In our work settings it is normal that teams may have already established some form of relationship, may have worked on other teams, and may go quickly and relatively painlessly toward maturity.

It is still a useful framework to consider your own development. Read through the description of these stages and then ask yourselves, "Where are we in this process?"

FORMING

In the first stages of team building, the *forming* of the team takes place. The team meets and learns about the opportunity and challenges, agrees on goals, and begins to tackle the tasks. Team members tend to behave quite independently. They may be motivated but are usually relatively uninformed of the issues and objectives of the team. Team members are usually on their best behavior but very focused on themselves. Mature team members begin to model appropriate behavior even at this early phase.

Leaders of the team tend to need to be directive during this phase.

The forming stage of any team is important because in this stage the members of the team get to know one another and make new friends. This is also a good opportunity to see how each member of the team works as an individual and how each responds to pressure. Trust is being established, and this will be the basis of their future work.

STORMING

Groups are then likely to enter the *storming* stage in which different ideas and individuals compete for consideration. The team addresses issues such as what problems they are really supposed to solve, how they will function independently and together and what leadership model they will accept. Team members open up to each other and confront each other's ideas and perspectives.

In some cases *storming* can be resolved quickly. In others, the team never leaves this stage. The maturity of some team members usually determines whether the team will ever move out of this stage. Some team members will focus on minutiae to evade real issues.

NORMING

At some point, the team may enter the *norming* stage. Team members adjust their behavior to each other as they develop work habits that make teamwork seem more natural and fluid. Team members often work through this stage by agreeing on rules, values, professional behavior, shared methods, working tools and even taboos. During this phase, team members begin to trust each other. Motivation increases as the team gets more acquainted with the project or process for which the team is responsible.

Teams in this phase may lose their creativity if the norming behaviors become too strong and begin to stifle healthy dissent and the team begins to exhibit groupthink.

PERFORMING

Hopefully, your team will reach the *performing* stage. These high-performing teams are able to function as a unit as they find ways to get the job done smoothly and effectively without inappropriate conflict or the need for external supervision. Team members have become interdependent. By this time they are motivated and knowledgeable. The team members are now competent, autonomous and able to handle the decision-making process without supervision. Dissent is expected and allowed as long as it is channeled through means acceptable to the team.

Leaders of the team during this phase are almost always participative. The facilitation of the team may now rotate among members. The team will make most of the necessary decisions. Even the most high-performing teams will revert to earlier stages in certain circumstances. Many long-standing teams will go through these cycles many times as they react to changing circumstances. For example, a change in leadership may cause the team to revert to *storming* as the new people challenge the existing norms and dynamics of the team.

TEAM MATURITY AND DECISION-MAKING

Another way to understand the maturing of a team is to consider the degree to which the team takes responsibility for its own performance.

When a team acts as a true business owner, initiating action to communicate with customers and suppliers, measuring its own performance, and acting with self-initiative to make improvements, it may be said to have high "performance initiative." Many teams when they are first formed are waiting to be told what to do. They are looking to do what is acceptable, not to initiate improvements.

If you look at the next diagram, you will see a matrix with Performance Initiative on one axis. On the other axis is the control of decisions – who is making the decisions? An easy way to think of this is to think about a child growing into adolescence, and then into mature adulthood. Every parent has struggled with the issue of how much freedom to allow a teenager. Of course, every teenager wants more freedom to decide when to come home at night, whom to associate with, etc. How does the parent know when to let go and "delegate" these kinds of decisions to the young person? The answer lies in performance. The more maturely teenagers behave, the more reasonable it is to allow them to make their own decisions. The parent moves through a progression from telling, through advising, to delegating.

What happens if the parent gives up control of decision-making too soon? This can lead to poor performance. The teens may not be ready to make their own decisions and may be likely to make unwise ones. Or, what happens if the teens are ready to make their own decisions, but the parent is over-controlling? This is de-motivating to the young person and is likely to lead to rebellious behavior.

Teams are not that different. When teams take responsibility for their own performance, the manager should assert less control and delegate more. On the other hand, if the team fails to take ownership of its performance or fails to initiate improvement efforts, the manager has a responsibility to be more directive.

What sometimes happens when implementing teams is that

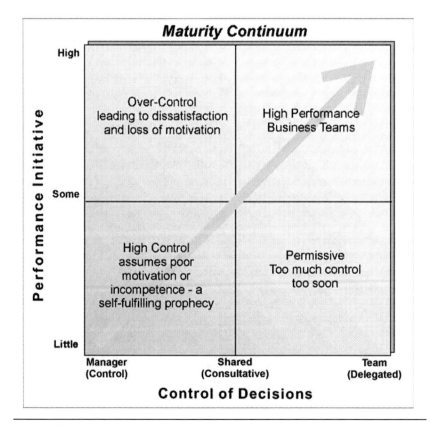

the manager is told that he "is supposed to let go." So he does, even though he may be very uncomfortable with this. His gut may have told him the truth, that the team was not ready to take responsibility on its own. This is a common cause of failure. Of course, failure also occurs because of over-control and the subsequent de-motivation of the team.

A human life progresses from dependence through independence to interdependence. In other words an infant, when born, is entirely dependent on the parents. Human beings are one of the least independent of infants. Fish are more capable at birth. But, as the infant matures in childhood she gains degrees of independence, walking, feeding, and learning to dress herself. The primary characteristic of teenagers is their declaration of independence – "I can do it myself!" But, that is not yet maturity. When you enter marriage you enter an agreement to be interdependent. In maturity individuals, teams, even companies and countries recognize the need for close collaboration, mutual interests, and development of the behavior required for effective interdependence.

Interdependence ⟹ *Adulthood*

Teams collaborate with SMEs and other functional areas to make decisions that are in the best interest of the whole business.

Independence ⟹ *Adolescence*

Workers exert autonomy of the team and begin to take control of performance. They act in the best interest of the team, but don't necessarily think about how the team's actions affect overall business performance and do not involve "outsiders" to help make the best decisions.

Dependence ⟹ *Childhood*

Workers depend on managers to worry about the overall performance output of the team. Workers are only concerned that they do *their* job well, and that their personal needs are met.

One of the more challenging issues when implementing Team Management is the change in management behavior and responsibilities as the teams mature. When teams are just beginning to develop it is incumbent on the immediate manager to make day-to-day decisions regarding work schedules, assignments, and problems. Many front line supervisors have been doing the same job for many years and have great difficulty believing that these functions can be taken over by the team. It is reasonable that they have a "show-me" attitude.

Training is not sufficient to make this transition. It is important to have on-site coaches who can give immediate feedback to both the teams and to the front line managers. The manager's job must be redesigned, and the manager is likely to need help making the transition to his new role, just as will the teams.

CHAPTER *8*

CLARIFYING DECISION STYLES AND PROCESS

A true lean culture is one in which decision-making at the lowest level is maximized, decisions are made quickly, and consensus decision-making is valued. When teams are empowered and clear in their responsibility they are capable of making many decisions on-the-spot and speeding improvement.

Sometimes rapid decision-making is best. However, sometime taking more time to reach consensus among a large number of people is a worthwhile investment.

One day I received a phone call from the Executive Vice President of Honda America Manufacturing, Scott Whitlcok. In my book, *American Spirit*, which they were using, I promoted *The Consensus Principle* as one of the keys to high performing companies. The VP asked me "Larry, what percent of the people do we need to have a consensus."

I had no idea what he was talking about, so I asked, "Well, how many people do you have?"

He replied that they had about ten thousand people. A bit surprised that he was trying to get a consensus from ten thousand people, I then asked, "Well, what is the decision on which you are trying to get consensus?"

"The drug policy" he replied.

Still a bit surprised, I then asked, "Well how many people are in agreement now?" He said that more than eight thousand were in agreement.

I then told him that I thought that was pretty good considering the number of people and nature of the question. But, that didn't satisfy him. He said that they were going to go through another round of involving the associates to reach consensus.

Honda is one of the world's best organizations. I am not saying that a 100% of employees need to agree on this or any other policy. However, this demonstrates their commitment to the principle of consensus. This doesn't mean that all decisions should be consensus, even on a team. Some decisions are better made as "command" or "consultative" decisions.

Members of a team want to understand how decisions are made and who makes them. Many of the conflicts that arise around teams involve a failure to clarify this decision process. If team members think they are going to make a decision, and a manager then makes the decision alone, they will be upset even if they agree with the decision. Disunity results from differing expectations and feeling betrayed that an agreement isn't being followed.

In my own company we had a once a month team meeting when all of the consultants and administrative staff would meet for the day, would share learning, discuss the company's finances, marketing, etc. More than once, I would put an issue before the

group and ask for input. Frequently, one of the consultants would ask me, "Larry, are you asking us for input so you can make the decision, or are you asking us to reach a consensus and make the decision?" Good question. Sometimes I wasn't sure and needed to clarify this in my own mind. Several times, I asked them whether they thought I should make the decision or let the group reach a decision. On most of those occasions, they preferred that I make the decision after listening to their input. They didn't want to spend the time to reach a consensus. It is not true that team members want to be involved in making every decision, but they do want input, and they want to know how those decisions are made.

Here is a quick primer on assigning decision responsibility: Consider three types of decisions: *Command, consultative* and *consensus.* The criteria for deciding which to use are *who knows, who cares, who acts, when must it be made?* The answer to these questions determines how decisions should be made.

COMMAND DECISIONS

Command decisions are those made by an individual. Individual command authority is not dead and not merely a left over dinosaur of the Roman Legions. Of course, command worked well on the battlefield on which quick decisions were required and obedience won battles. Even today, if the building is burning down, if the machine is spitting smoke and oil, if the customer calls and is furious that he got the wrong material delivered – is the right answer to call a meeting? Definitely not! These are decisions in which speed is more important than reaching consensus. These decisions are best left to individuals who are on-the-spot and have expert knowledge.

Speed and expert knowledge are two reasons for command to be the preferred decision style. In the operating room, with the patient cut open and the cardiologist holding a heart in his hand that has just stopped beating – do you want him to call a meeting to achieve a consensus decision? Not if it's your heart! Of course, you want him to use his expert knowledge and make a decision, fast! The greater the degree of knowledge an individual has compared to others on a team, the more likely a command decision is appropriate. The greater the required speed, the more likely it is that command decision-making is appropriate.

An organization in which command decision-making is predominant is an organization that lives in frequent crisis. This raises serious questions about the ability of the leaders to plan, engage in systematic action, and develop the people below them. Or it is an organization dominated by personalities whose egos prevent them from letting go of decisions and trusting others. Predominance of command decision-making reflects low trust and will soon de-motivate employees.

CONSULTATIVE OR SHARED DECISIONS

Consultative decisions involve selective involvement by those who know, care, or must act. If the customer calls and was shipped the wrong order, you may say, "I am very sorry about that. Let me look into it and call you back within an hour. We will definitely solve the problem." The customer will likely say "fine." The customer does not want to be told it will be taken up at the weekly meeting. And it is likely that you personally do not have sufficient information to know what to do to solve the problem on your own.

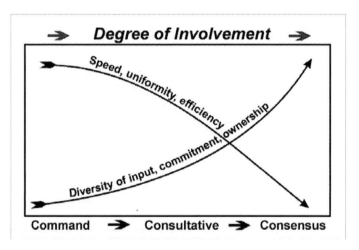

What you are likely to do, and this will make sense, is that you will then gather the two or three people who have knowledge, who may have some investment in this decision (they care), and who may have to take action to solve the problem. You can do this quickly. You will give them the facts and ask them what they think should be done to meet this customer's needs now. You are not trying to solve a systemic or process problem. You are just trying to fix this problem now. You are consulting with associates, but you are going to make a decision quickly, rather than turn the decision over to the team. This is consultative decision-making.

CONSENSUS DECISIONS

Consensus decisions are true team decisions where you turn over the decision to the group. The decision is then owned by the group. Consensus decisions involve a cost – the cost of time, energy, and the risk that you may not like the decision.

When do you employ consensus decision-making? First, when the conditions of speed and individual expertise are not the most important factors. You employ consensus when the quality of the decision, commitment, and unified action are most important; when the "who knows, who cares and who must act" includes the group.

Consensus is generally worth the investment for those decisions that involve long-term goals, and how we do things, our ongoing processes. All members of the group have an investment in the goals of the group and the "how" and "why" we do our work.

Involvement in these types of decisions gains commitment, gains the wisdom of the group, and provides for shared learning.

Ask your team which decisions should be command, consultative or consensus. You can create a great deal of clarity and have the group focus on those things that add most value for the group. The time and energy of teams is often wasted with trivial and inappropriate decisions. Use common sense.

CHAPTER *9*

Defining Customers, Suppliers and Process

When writing your team's charter you defined your suppliers, input, process, output and customers (SIPOC). However, you most likely did this in a relatively quick and general way. At this point in the process of developing your team you will want to do this in a more deliberate, specific and serious manner. You will be asked to follow through and act on these decisions. You will be asked to gather data from your customers, provide feedback to your suppliers, and you will map and study your work processes.

THE JOY IN WORK

Dr. Deming spoke of creating "joy" in work. He was serious and it was a thoughtful point that he was making. There is joy in work when it is done in the spirit of service to someone else. There is joy in work when you feel that you have control over the quality of your work. There is even more joy in work when you know that you are expert and that you are daily striving to improve the quality of your work. All work should have joy. The process of *Lean Team Management* can bring that joy to your work. In this chapter, you will begin to establish those conditions that create joy, or the simple satisfaction of knowing that you are doing your work well.

The basic functions of a team are to...

- Define your customers and their requirements for the work you deliver to them.
- To define your work process that creates the output of products or services that goes to your customer.
- To receive feedback on your work and to strive to continuously improve your work process and results.
- To become the "world's greatest experts" in the work you do.
- To provide feedback to your suppliers, who provide the input that you need to do your work in the best possible way.

DEFINING THE IMPORTANT FUNCTIONS OF A WORK OR MANAGEMENT TEAM

The real work of organizations is horizontal, not vertical. We often think of the work we do as being for our manager, in other words, going up the organization. But the real work that organizations do that result in revenue and profit flows horizontally through the organization to a customer. Almost every organization is a series of work processes, that transform input received from a supplier, to output delivered to a customer. High performing organizations are passionately focused on managing this flow of work, this core work process that creates the real value of the organization. All the work of managers and staff should be designed to enhance the work of the teams that manage this core work process.

WHO ARE OUR CUSTOMERS?

Who receives the work of your team? Who cares about the work of your team? Who makes use of the work of your team? Who pays for the work product of your team? The answer to these questions is the answer to the question "who are your customers?"

When thinking about your customers, you are likely to ask, "Can customers be inside the company, or must they be the end-use customer who pays money to our company?" The answer is "yes, both." In most organizations work is a chain of teams, linked together to serve external customers. The final customer is only served as well as the performance of the weakest link on the chain.

WHAT IS OUR OUTPUT THAT ADDS VALUE?

What does your team produce that serves the needs of your customers? In the next chapter we will do a more detailed analysis of customer requirements and prepare to interview customers. Now, make a list of what you regard as the most important products or services that are the result of the work of your team. Think about more than the product, the "stuff" that gets delivered. It is very often the case that what differentiates one company or team from another is "how" they deliver, the service component, or the knowledge and information that is shared.

WHAT INPUT DO WE NEED TO ADD VALUE?

In order to do your work you need things. You need materials, money, people, training, information, or other things. What are the inputs that your team requires to do your work? Again, this input may come from a work cell next to yours, or it may come from a company far away.

WHO ARE OUR SUPPLIERS?

Your team is the customer of other teams. They are your suppliers. You should consider both internal and external suppliers. For each of the inputs you identified above, there should be a corresponding supplier.

WHAT IS OUR CORE WORK PROCESS?

Your core work process will be the focus of your efforts to improve. It is the core work process that will produce the output that goes to your customers. Your team members should be the "world's greatest experts" in their own core work process.

If you are unsure what your core work process is, ask yourself the following questions:

- What would most interrupt the work of the organization if we stopped doing it?
- What do we really get paid for? Why do they give us a check?
- What is the work that we do that is part of the larger flow of work that serves end-use customers who pay money to our organization?

CORE VERSUS ENABLING PROCESSES

In every organization there are both core and enabling processes. The organization cannot succeed without both. Enabling processes enhance and "enable" the core work process. For example, if you are an advertising agency, your core work is writing, developing, creating great advertisements. But, everyone in the organization does not directly work on advertisements. Some people do accounting for the organization. Some people are human resource specialists who do hiring, provide training, manage compensation, etc. These are enabling processes. If you are an accounting firm, then accounting done for clients, who pay you to do that accounting, is a core work process.

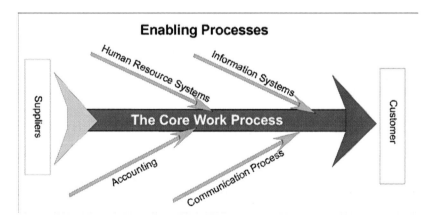

The measure of the effectiveness of enabling processes is how well they serve the core work process. In other words, the customers for those doing enabling processes, are those who work on the core work process. Everything the organization does must ultimately enhance the value of the output we provide to our customers.

Why is it important to make this distinction? Because sometimes teams and organizations lose focus, and doing things that are supposed to be enabling actually becomes a distraction to the core work.

THE POWER OF FEEDBACK

All teams, all people, require feedback for their performance to improve. Feedback is the information we receive that tells us that our performance is increasing, decreasing, or the same. It is a primary source of motivation to change. It is why we step on a scale to weigh ourselves. It is why we attend sports events and are continually looking up to the scoreboard. It is why stock charts and tickers are so popular. It is why we have to keep our eyes on the road when we are driving, so we will know if we are drifting to one side or the other and correct. Feedback keeps us on track. All people need feedback in regard to all performance that matters.

Work or management teams need feedback for all the same reasons that sports teams need feedback. Where does it come from? Basically, there are only three ways we get feedback: first, we generate measures of performance within the team; second we receive feedback from above; and third, we receive feedback from those who receive our work, our customers.

The purpose of this SIPOC model is to establish sources of feedback that will guide our behavior and increase our ability to be

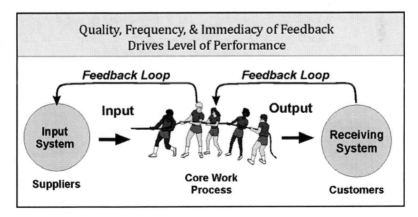

self-managing. And, this is the same reason we need to help our suppliers by giving them feedback.

CHAPTER *10*

DEFINING CUSTOMER REQUIREMENTS

I have worked with many leadership teams and asked the question *"What do you do as a team that adds value to your customers?"* Very often members of the team will then respond by referring to the product or service that their company sells to their customers. I then ask *"Does this team make or provide that service?"* Of course they don't. I then repeat the question…*"What do you do as a team that adds value to your customers?"* Often, there is then a pregnant pause as they ponder exactly what they do as a team that adds value. Then, it slowly comes. They do add value. They develop strategy. They do things that influence and direct the culture of the organization. They allocate resources.

Too often leadership teams have not defined their work in terms of how they add value and therefore, they do a lot of things that are waste. By focusing on how they add value, and getting feedback from their customers, they can improve the quality of their decisions, the use of their time, and their functioning as a team. It is also important that the leadership establish the model of defining and listening to customers. Be the change you want for your organization!

Who is the world's greatest expert on customer satisfaction? That is an easy question. Of course, it is the customer, and no one else. So we will go to the customer to find out.

TYPES OF CUSTOMER REQUIREMENTS

What kinds of information do we want to know from our customer? The following can help you think about the kinds of questions you will ask the customer:

SPECIFICATIONS

What specifications does the customer care about? This may include actual dimensions; tolerances between components; weight of the product; surface characteristics such as smoothness or color; or any other measures.

RELIABILITY

Some of your products or services may perfectly match the customer specifications. However, every customer demands reliability of the product as well. That will include the frequency of out-of-spec units and the reliability of service or customer interface transactions. In other words, not answering the phone is a reliability problem. It says, "I can't rely on this company (person or team)."

TIMELINESS

We have become a "just-in-time" society. We order movies and expect them delivered to our mailbox the next day or we download them for immediate viewing. We have incredible expectations for things being delivered on time, every time. What are your customer's requirements for timeliness of product or service delivery?

COURTESY

Included in courtesy is not just "being nice" but listening well, responding to what the customer is saying, and genuinely having empathy, understanding for the customer's needs. Most customers are willing to forgive errors, but have much more trouble forgiving a supplier who refuses to understand the problem they may be causing. We all want to work with other people, either on our team, or with customers and suppliers, who demonstrate genuine understanding of our needs.

INNOVATION

Another requirement that many customers have, particularly in service companies, is for ways of doing things that are innovative. We like to work with suppliers who are not standing still, but are continually developing better ways to do things. The way your customer views you has a lot to do with how innovative you are. Customers like to be surprised, not by just meeting what they tell you their needs are, but by your company or team inventing ways of serving them that they had not imagined before.

HOW TO GATHER DATA FROM YOUR CUSTOMERS

You will have to decide the best way for you to gather information from your customers. You will have to consider the time and resources required and the importance of different customers. You will want to prioritize your customers and be sure to gather information from those who are most important to your team or company.

There is a temptation to rely on the most simple and quickest way to gather customer feedback. This is certainly a written questionnaire or web-based survey. However, this is usually not the most effective way. It is very common for a team to end up with a lot of paper or bytes of data that is poorly analyzed and leads to little understanding. Face-to-face interviews, even if they involve fewer customers, are usually the most meaningful. When a customer looks you in the eye and explains a problem or a need, you feel something that motivates change. Staring at paper rarely does the same.

CUSTOMER QUESTIONNAIRES

A customer questionnaire is probably the least expensive way of gathering information. However, it is also the way that is likely to produce the lowest response rate (the number returned), and it does not provide the opportunity for you to listen to explanations, reflect on those explanations, and ask clarifying questions.

Questionnaires should not be too long. I have received questionnaires that I wanted to fill out, but by the time I got to the fourth page of questions, I just decided that I didn't have the time for it. Questionnaires need to prioritize the most important questions and allow the customer to reply promptly.

TELEPHONE INTERVIEWS

Telephone interviews have the advantage of allowing you to listen carefully and to ask clarifying questions ("what was it about that experience that was most helpful?"). It is also less expensive than a face-to-face interview because you do not have to travel.

When conducting telephone interviews, or face-to-face interviews, it is very helpful if two people conduct the interview together. One person can focus on asking the questions, including follow-up questions, while the other person concentrates on writing down or recording the information. It is very hard to do both of these things well, at the same time.

FACE-TO-FACE INTERVIEWS

Face-to-face interviews have the additional advantage of allowing you to read body language and to develop a relationship with the customer. Very often, by watching the customer's facial expressions, you will be prompted to ask clarifying questions. For example, you may see the customers roll their eyes, or throw their heads back, signs of frustration, and you might then say "It seems like that is something that has caused you frustration. Can you tell me more about that?"

Do not underestimate the importance of developing a personal relationship with your customers. Friendship and trust go a long way toward improving customer satisfaction. One customer being interviewed by a team, who had been very unhappy with the service they had received from an internal department, was asked at the end of the interview, "Is there anything else we can do for you?" And, he replied by saying "Well, you have just done the most important thing you can do. You have listened to me. I didn't think you people ever listened to us. It makes a big difference." While the purpose of the interview was not to change customer satisfaction, the process of face-to-face conversation did change the relationship. It began to create trust.

Note: in the corresponding chapter in *Lean Team Management,* the workbook, there is a more specific guide to developing customer interviews, analyzing the data, and practicing interviewing skills. This book, being an overview, will not repeat this.

CHAPTER *11*

Developing Your Team Scorecard

Just as for every other team, the leadership team should develop a scorecard that reflects their contribution to the organization.

Keeping score, taking a count, must be the oldest of all practices of management. Everything that works is not new, and some of the best things are old. Keeping score is as old as the most ancient sport and the most ancient business. Motivation hasn't changed that much in thousands of years.

Management can be fun. Ownership of a business or work process is fun. It is fun for the same reasons that playing sports is fun - keeping score, having the numbers, feeling that it is your team, and that you can influence winning and losing.

But things are more easily said than done. In many organizations teams are not structured to provide ownership of clear business processes. Teams must be structured to own a business process that can be the focus of "their business" and scorecard. Lean Team Management creates a team structure with accountability for performance and makes the adult-to-adult assumption that employees and manager are mature, do want to take responsibility for improving business performance, and, if given the information and structure, will rise to that responsibility. This assumption has rarely proven false.

Some years ago my consultants and I were implementing a team process at Eastman Chemicals in Kingsport, Tennessee. I vividly remember a discussion with a department manager when we suggested that financial information on the performance of first level work teams be shared with those teams so they could take responsibility for their business performance. The department manager thought that was ridiculous. He said with great authority "You don't understand these people. These people don't care about that information. They work here just to get their pay check and go home. In fact, you ought to know that most of them consider this their second job."

This was puzzling since this "second job" was eight hours a day, at least five days a week. I asked, "So what do they consider their first job, if this is their second job?"

He replied "Well, most of them have their own farms, or some other business that they run. That's what they really care about."

This raised a disturbing question. "What causes these employees to feel more motivation about their own farms or small company then working at Eastman Chemicals?"

That led me to ask this department manager, "Do you think they look at the revenue and cost numbers for their first job?"

"Of course, most of them do their own accounting. They know exactly how well they are doing," he replied.

"Do you think they talk to their customers and are concerned about their satisfaction?" I asked. "Of course, they make darn sure they can sell their produce or product, it's their business."

So these same employees who consider this their "second job" and don't care about the numbers, in their other job, they run the business, do the accounting, take responsibility for sales, marketing, quality management, process improvement, and everything else that goes into running a business. This only proves that most often motivation is not simply in the person, but is in the system that surrounds the person.

Hundreds, if not thousands, of times I have seen the person change from someone who "just wants a paycheck" to someone who feels and acts like a business owner and manager, not because they received a personality transplant, but because of relatively simple changes in the nature of the system that surrounds them. The essence of that change has always been giving them genuine responsibility for managing a piece of the business, with the information, the authority to make decisions, and the accountability for performance inherent in the assumption of being a "business manager."

SCOREKEEPING IS A SYSTEM OF MOTIVATION

Dr. Deming used to say that when he visited a manufacturing plant, he wanted to see graphs posted, and he wanted to see dirty fingerprints on the graph. No fingerprints – no good! Why? He wanted to know that those doing the work were literally in touch with the results of their work, their score. Many thought this was a simplistic and foolish idea, but perhaps Dr. Deming understood the same common sense that every team and every coach understands.

The next time you watch a football, baseball, or basketball game have a notepad in your lap and write down every measurement, every kind of score, that is mentioned. When you reach fifty in one game, you can quit. In all cases there is a constant reference to numbers. Most of the references are about positive, not negative, numbers – the most balls hit over the fence in right field, the most three pointers shot by a left-handed shooter in the fourth quarter of a game! They seem to have scores on everything.

Scorekeeping is also a system that creates unity in groups. Imagine the scoreboard at a basketball or football game – everyone watches it, everyone cheers when it changes, and without it there

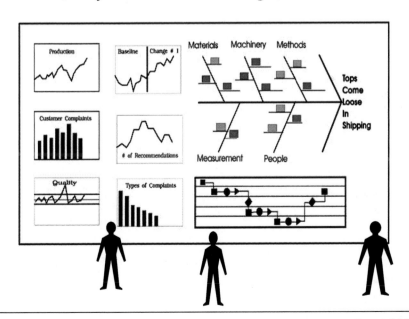

would be no fans in the stands. What is the magic of the scoreboard? If you understand this, then you understand how to create great scorekeeping systems at work. Something about the way we are internally wired causes us to derive great pleasure in seeing the numbers change; watching the ball go through the hoop, everyone cheers; then their eyes turn to the scoreboard, and they are pleased with the change in score. The entire process helps to bond the team and fans together.

Even those who have no reason to motivate others, but only to motivate themselves, create scorekeeping systems. For example, the lonely runners – those who are able to maintain this behavior for years -- almost all have established a scorekeeping system that keeps them going; minutes per mile; miles per day, week and month; pulse rate after one or five miles. There are dozens of ways to keep score, and those who maintain their motivation maintain a scorekeeping system. It is the single most obvious essence of self-management.

Scorekeeping has gone through numerous iterations and fads. From the management-by-objectives of the 1950's and 60's to the current statistical standards of quality, they all derive their power from the simple impact of feedback and knowledge of performance. The results that have been achieved from Total Quality Management, statistical process control, or Six Sigma are not only the result of computing statistics. The majority of the effect is the feedback effect, and it comes from the simple practice of creating systematic scorekeeping.

KEYS TO EFFECTIVE SCOREKEEPING

Here are the keys to scorekeeping.

IMMEDIACY AND FREQUENCY:

In basketball, the fans look up at the scoreboard and expect to see a change in one to three seconds after the ball goes through the hoop. In baseball, perhaps because they don't score that often, they have from two to ten seconds. After that amount of time, in either sport, the fans get itchy and may start to show their frustration. If it took an hour to get the score up on the board, how would the fans and players feel? Quickly they would lose motivation and would not show up for the game. How long do your employees or team members wait? The speed and frequency of feedback both increase motivation and increase the effect of a shared experience, and bonding.

Almost every organization can improve motivation simply by increasing the rate and frequency of feedback. In most organizations, the only reason feedback is delayed is that no one has worked at creating a frequent and immediate feedback system. Investors watch the "real time" ticker and graphs of their investments as they change by the minute or second. With computer technology, creating this kind of feedback is not difficult; we simply need to do it.

Some may fear that this kind of feedback will cause employees to lose sight of longer-term goals and become distracted by random fluctuations in data. It is for this reason that all feedback systems should not overly focus on one variable, but should present a data array, five to eight variables that vary in type of data and frequency.

VARIETY

Of course, not all scores can be delivered in seconds. Some scores (monthly sales, quarterly financials) can only be computed in much longer cycles. This is also true in sports. Some scores are annual or career numbers (earned run average over years or career, annual batting average, current batting average, etc.) and many other scores are for that day's game. This is characteristic of all effective motivational systems. Design your scorekeeping system to include individual and team, short-term and long-range scores. But be sure that the information is delivered as quickly as possible to those who perform. Remember, it is not just the fans in the stand (stockholders, analysts, management) that need the information; it is those on the playing field.

VISIBILITY

The United Way gets it. They place a big thermometer graph right at the entrance to the building where you cannot possibly miss it. And every day as you pass it, you don't know why, but you get some little satisfaction in seeing it move up toward its goal. United Way understands the power of good scorekeeping – or good feedback systems.

Visiting the Honda America Manufacturing plant for the first time about ten or twelve years ago, I noticed the complete lack of artwork on the walls. Just as well – there was little room on the walls for artwork – they were almost all covered with charts and graphs! They know feedback systems. We think about what we see. We see data, we think about data. We see our scores going up; we react to those scores going up, or down!

Beginning in the early 1970s, I was involved in implementing behavior change and performance improvement programs in manufacturing plants. The idea of graphing and charting performance, visually displaying the ups and downs of a team's performance, was a new thing in most manufacturing plants. Virtually every time performance was visually graphed for a team to see and understand, performance improved. It is the "no-brainer" of performance improvement.

OWNERSHIP

We are excited by a change in numbers when we feel those numbers are for "my team," when we have ownership of that performance, even if it isn't a direct reflection of our own performance. We don't have to be the athlete, but we do have to feel that it is *our team*. And, if we are the athlete, the one performing, we bloody well want measures of our performance, and not someone else's.

It is common for teams to give themselves a name, create their own logo or mascot, and have some piece of clothing made with their team's logo. It is a normal thing to want to identify with a team, root for a team, and follow the scores of a team. There is no reason why all of this cannot be part of your company's work environment. Imagine any environment in which individuals or teams put forth maximum effort, achieve maximum results, and have fun while they are at it. Inevitably, there will be extremely clear scorekeeping, immediate feedback, and visual display of the score.

BALANCED

We have come a long way. There was a time when some managers felt that the only thing that mattered was financial results. Those who wanted to elevate the importance of quality measures, customer satisfaction, or the performance of processes had to do battle (and usually lost!) with the financial managers.

Two things have worked to alter the view of most managers today. The first is the surge by Japanese car companies and the adoption of the quest for quality by most major U.S. corporations. These have elevated the understanding of quality and process measures. Almost all managers understand that the way you get to financial measures is through effective processes and quality. The second is the book by Kaplan & Norton[7] that promoted the idea of a balanced scorecard and succeeded in arguing for a system of balanced measures in the organization.

Following is a diagram that illustrates the possible components of a balanced scorecard. Kaplan and Norton emphasize that their model and definition of a balanced scorecard is not

Team Balanced Scorecard

Customer Satisfaction

Learning & Development

Strategy, Vision and Values

Business Processes Performance

Financial Results

something fixed in stone, but a proposal that they expect others to modify, adapt, and evolve with their own needs and experience.

Any scorekeeping process should account for process improvement and people development as well as financial and

---

[7] Kaplan, Robert S., Norton, David P. *The Balanced Scorecard: Translating Strategy into Action.* Harvard Business School Press, Boston, 1997.

customer satisfaction results. When developing a scorekeeping process, the team should identify those questions that will lead to learning and development. For an athletic team, for example, they might ask, "How many seconds does the quarterback take to release the ball? How many seconds does it take the receivers to run the twenty yard dash down field?" The answers to these questions will provide the specific feedback that will promote learning. Learning will not result from looking at the team score at the end of the game. The learning will come from the components of team performance.

BUILDING YOUR SCORECARD

Everything that follows is a suggestion as to how to construct your balanced scorecard. Think! You may think of a better way, of variables that are more important, or a better process. But, the following are steps that have proven to work in other organizations and are a pretty good starting point for your own thoughts.

The process is as important as the decisions. The results are in the process. The following five steps to develop each measure should work for you.

1. DEFINE THE SCORE

For each variable, for specifications for example, there may be dozens of specifications for your product. It can be measured a hundred ways. But from your interviews with customers, you learned something about which specifications are most important. Define the few specifications that are most important to customer satisfaction.

When developing your team scorecard, you do not want to have twenty different scores. You want to have four to eight (approximately) scores that are a balanced representation of your team's performance. It is almost always true that, if a team selects twenty different scores, in a short time they will lose track of them and not plot their data on a consistent basis. Constancy of purpose is important when developing your scorecard. Be realistic.

2. BASELINE DATA

How do you know when you have improved? Before you seek improvement, it is very helpful to have baseline data that will give you a basis to determine whether or not you are making changes that are paying off.

Below you will see a graph with baseline data recorded and then the data after the team has made a change in their work process. You can see that the baseline performance is stable. This is important because if there is already an upward trend in performance, how will you know that a new change is making a difference? It is better to let that trend play out; let it get to the point of achieving stability. Then you can implement a change to your process and you will be able to see the difference.

Most importantly, notice how easy it is to see the point of improvement on the graph. Clearly whatever the team did made a positive difference. By seeing the change occur on the graph after they have made a change, the team is learning. They are learning by using the scientific method, which is simply to know the facts of

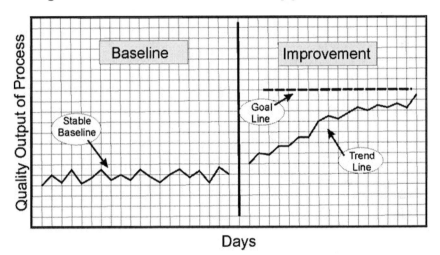

performance by collecting data, then making a change that might affect performance, and then observing the "post-intervention" data.

You can also see that there is a goal line on the graph. When a team sets a goal that they put on the graph, it gives them something to shoot for, something to celebrate when they succeed. Again, seeing it on the graph is extremely helpful to motivate the team.

3. SET OBJECTIVES

We are not talking about "management-by-objectives here. We are talking about YOUR team setting objectives for YOUR own performance. It is the difference between being "managed" and "self-managing." Look at the graph of your performance. Then look at what improvements you think you need to make based on the feedback you received from your customers. In later chapters, we will discuss problem-solving methods that will help you make these improvements.

4. CHANGE

In later chapters you will look more thoroughly at specific problems you will find in your process and institute changes. Your period of implementing changes may be days or months. The important thing is that you are going to plot your data and keep track of the effect of your changes as a team.

5. EVALUATE

The focus of your team meetings should be on this scorecard, what you are doing to improve it, and watching your data. You should be discussing whether or not your changes are having the desired affect and whether or not the data is stable or trending in one direction or another.

THE MAJOR COMPONENTS OF THE SCORECARD

In the preceding diagram you will see five components of the scorecard. In the center are Strategy, Vision and Values. Your scores should support or reinforce the strategy of the organization. Your team leader, who is part of the management team above, should assure that you are measuring things that will help the organization achieve its strategic goals.

CUSTOMER SATISFACTION:

These are the same variables you included when you interviewed your customers.

1. Specifications
2. Reliability
3. Timeliness
4. Courtesy
5. Innovation

PROCESS PERFORMANCE:

In the next chapter we will work on defining your team's work processes. After you do that, it will make sense to return to this section of your scorecard and see if you wish to make any changes or additions.

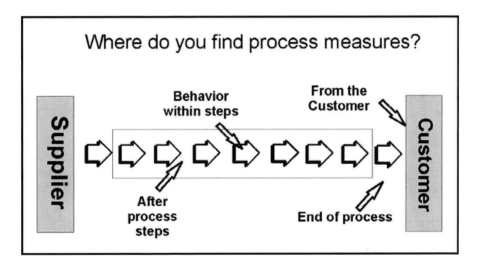

1. Cycle Time

Every process has a cycle time. A process begins at a point in time, and it ends at a later point in time. In a factory you can measure when incoming chemicals, wires, and other inputs arrive at the loading dock to enter a warehouse or the production process. The period from arrival until they leave the facility as a completed product defines the complete production cycle time. You can then measure what percent of this time the material is actually being transformed from incoming state to outgoing state. Of course, the value-adding time is a fraction of the actual cycle time. The ratio of value-adding to non-value-adding time is a measure of waste in the system.

You can do the exact same thing in an office or knowledge work environment. Projects, reports, and studies all have a cycle time, and much of that cycle time is non-value-adding time. It is waste, and much of it can be eliminated.

2. Reliability

You discussed and selected a customer satisfaction measure for reliability as products or services are received by the customer. However, you are expert in your own process. You may see that your process breaks down and has interruptions or errors that are never seen by your customer. Even though these are not seen by the customer, these reliability problems may cost you time and money.

3. Productivity

Before the quality movement became a primary focus of managers, the productivity movement was the key driver of improvement. The concept of productivity is no less relevant today than it was in years past. Productivity measures should be included in your balanced scorecard.

Productivity is a measure of the output of a process or organization, divided by the input required to produce that output. For example, an auto assembly plant may require fifteen person-hours of labor to assemble a car. Another assembly plant may require twenty hours of labor to assemble a similar car. It is reasonable to say that the system or process of assembly at the first plant is more productive than the second. This will, of course, result in a cost advantage. That cost may be redeployed to other areas, such as research, updating equipment, etc. You can also measure productivity in terms of dollars spent on production in relation to dollars paid for the product. Or, materials input to the process relative to the output.

4. Variability

It is generally true that the less variability in an operation or process, the higher will be the quality. Variability tends to introduce waste in the form of re-doing or re-adjusting. Variability sometimes indicates that we do not really know how to do things. There are two kinds of variability. One kind is introduced by external requirements. For example, you may be completing grant proposals. Each grant has different requirements to which you must respond. This is externally imposed variability. The other kind of variability is created within the process. Sometimes this is desirable experimentation. But often, it is just not following procedure or having to deal with defective parts created in an earlier step in the process. Eliminating this kind of variability is eliminating waste.

5. Innovation

There are two kinds of innovation, and both are important to your organization. One is innovation in product or service, the output of the process. The other is innovation in the process itself.

The innovation that is most easily noticed by your customers is innovation in the nature of a product or service. Improvements in the product or service do not come only from engineers and those who design products and services. They also come from the recommendations of those who are on-the-spot, making the product or delivering the service.

FINANCIAL RESULTS:

In the not-so-good old days, financial matters were considered to be the business of upper level managers only. This was part of the class system that separated those doing the work from those supervising the work. This distinction probably made sense when workers were illiterate and didn't have access to the Internet. Today, the world's best companies are finding ways to share the "business game" with their employees so they also have the "joy" and anxiety, of monitoring financial performance.

Exactly what makes most sense in regard to financial scores is very dependent on the culture and operations of your organization. Every team will be somewhat different in this regard, and you will have to seek ways to develop financial measures for your team. But, remember that you are not really "managing" until you are accountable for revenue, costs, or utilization of assets. The real game of business must include a concern for financial performance.

LEARNING AND DEVELOPMENT

If we believe in continuous improvement we must recognize that continuous improvement must be not only in our process and products, but also in our people. How can we measure learning and development at the team level? The following four are potential categories of measurement for learning and development.

1. Skills

Every process requires a set of skills. This is true whether we are talking about a senior management team, an accounting team, or a front line team in a manufacturing plant. For every team, you should have an inventory of the skills required to optimize the performance of that team. For example, there may be maintenance skills, assembly skills, training skills, statistical analysis skills, computer skills, etc. These are different for every team.

2. Knowledge

Knowledge is different from skills, although they are usually related. Skills are things you do, behavior that can be performed, like singing or dancing. Knowledge is data in the data bank of the mind. You may have knowledge, but not have a corresponding skill. For example, you may read a book on playing the piano, or singing opera. You may have all the knowledge one could have, but you may still not be able to perform the skill. Knowledge can be tested with a paper and pencil test (or on the computer.)

3. Development Goals

This section refers to people development goals. It is a good practice for team leaders or managers to sit down each year (or more often) with each team member and give them feedback on ways in which they can personally develop. Each individual might have three or four developmental goals. A goal might include attending a training course or learning a new skill from other team members or a company trainer. You can have each team member share with the team how many goals they have and how many they have met during a year or a quarter. This will be some indication of the team's dedication to personal improvement.

4. Multi-Skills

Imagine a baseball team on which every player was fully capable of playing four or five positions. Every coach wants to have a "utility infielder" who can play any of the infield positions.

Imagine if they could also pitch and catch. These would be "multi-skilled" players. The ability to step in when another player is absent is a valuable asset to any team. It is generally a deliberate effort of team leaders to create as many multi-skilled players as possible. The ability to rotate jobs also increases job satisfaction and reduced boredom.

COMPLETING YOUR TEAM SCORECARD

The above categories scores may seem a bit overwhelming. Your team is not going to develop a scorecard for every possible variable. These categories and questions are simply a way to get the team members to think about what is important and possible in developing their scorecard.

Now it is time for your team to consult together, brainstorm together, and reach consensus together on the scores that would be most indicative of your team's performance.

Remember that you do not want more than four to eight scores that you monitor as a team. Also, please remember to make the score visible. Graph it!!! Post it on the wall where your team meets or works. Remember the scoreboard at the basketball game. Don't cover it up!

CHAPTER *12*

MAPPING YOUR TEAM'S PROCESSES

Let's be honest. Leadership teams rarely map their work processes. There is something too pedestrian about it. And it is for this reason that they often fail to learn and improve how they do things. I was coaching the senior leadership of one of the major oil companies. A point came when it was time to do the annual strategic planning. As they started to discuss who would do what to prepare the strategic plan, I asked "How did you do it last year and what did you learn from that experience." They confessed that it didn't go well last year and they weren't sure what they learned. I then facilitated as they mapped the desired process and we agreed to evaluate the process after it had been completed so that we could improve it for the following year. If you have to make up a process every time you do it, you will never get good at it. This is just as true for the most senior management team, as it is for the first level team.

Lean Management is about the flow of the work, from suppliers to customers, and creating the ideal flow that will add the most value for your customers and contain the least possible waste. The ideal process is so lacking in interruptions that it feels natural - it flows.

ACHIEVING "FLOW"

High performing teams or individuals appear *natural* when their performance flows with seemingly little effort. Athletes experience *flow*, or what they may call, "being in the zone." A musician may say she is in "the groove." Flow for an individual is complete focus, absorption in a task, when all energies move with ease and without interruption. Rather than feeling great exertion, the work feels natural and exhilarating. Mihaly Csikszentmihalyi described flow as the psychology of optimal experience. *"It is what the sailor holding a tight course feels when the wind whips through her hair, when the boat lunges through the waves like a colt – sail, hull, wind, and sea humming in a harmony that vibrates in the sailor's veins. It is what the painter feels when the colors on the canvas begin to set up a magnetic tension with each other, and a new thing, a living form, takes shape in front of the astonished creator."*[8]

If you have ever watched a great basketball team run the court on a fast break with each player having perfect confidence in the other, looking one way, and passing the ball another with certainty that the teammate will be there, and three quick passes around and over defenders ends in what looks like an effortless dunk through the hoop, you have observed flow.

This experience of flow is not a serendipitous surprise. The sailor has studied her course and angle to the wind, has set the right sail for the conditions, has practiced her hand on the tiller, and knows how her boat responds to this wind and these waves. The appearance of natural or effortless performance is the result of trained competence. The basketball team has practiced each motion a thousand times, knows that when it is two-on-one, or three-on-two, or whatever other combination, there are set patterns to run and each player trusts the other only because they have practiced this repeatedly. In each of these cases, the flow is a well-managed process, a series of steps that fit perfectly together and are acted out in perfect coordination. It is this studied combination of parts, which fit perfectly in a unified whole, and their perfect execution that create the sense of flow.

DEATH BY PROCESS!

---

[8] Csikszentmihalyi, Mihaly. Flow: The Psychology of Optimal Experience. New York. Harper Perennial, 1990. p. 3.

Processes can kill you and sometimes do. I don't know how many coroners' reports have said "Death by Process," but many should have.

My consultants and I were working with a large healthcare provider and had been given the assignment to "re-engineer" the core process in the organization. Of course, the core process was providing health care solutions to individuals and insurance clients. A design team was formed to study the core process and develop an improved solution to eliminate many well-known problems. The seriousness of those problems was sometimes buried under the routine of daily work.

The design team, after several months of work analyzing the process and developing a solution, made a presentation to the senior Executive Committee that included the company president. Because they were about to propose some fairly radical solutions, they were concerned that they get the executives' attention in a dramatic way. So, they dramatized a patient experience. They role-played a scenario in which one of their client members develops an unexplained stomach pain.

Her first stop is to her general practitioner and after filling out forms and sitting for an hour in the waiting room, she is told that she needs to see a specialist and is given a list of several specialists whom she could then call.

She already took off from work for her first appointment which added no value.

She goes home and gets on the phone. It will be a month before any of the specialists can see her. She makes an appointment.

She shows up a month later at the specialist's office. The specialist immediately tells her that he wants her to take a series of tests and she is referred to a clinic that provides the necessary tests. She calls and makes an appointment for two weeks later.

When she shows up at the clinic, she is informed that she has to get pre-approval from her insurance provider before they can administer these tests.

She goes home and calls the insurance provider.

You get the picture. The story was detailed and frustrating just listening to it, let alone if you had to go through it. The story ends, after months of wrong appointments, delays, and re-routing, in the doctor's office where she finds out that she has cancer and the doctor informs her that treatment could have been much more successful if she had come in sooner. She dies. In effect, *the process* murdered her.

The leader of the design team, to lighten up the somewhat somber mood in the meeting with the executives said, "Of course that story may be a bit exaggerated. Perhaps we don't kill people, but people do suffer through our system."

With that the president of the company, a doctor and healthcare executive for many years, interrupts. "Excuse me, but there is nothing exaggerated about that. That was my mother! That is exactly what happened to my mother."

A long and tense silence followed as everyone tried to figure out how to respond to that revelation. The president broke the silence and said, "Well, let's fix it!" Not surprisingly, they approved implementation of the redesigned process.

Isn't it odd that we handle packages with more efficiency and care than we do patients? And that is because package delivery companies have become much more focused on eliminating waste from their processes and assuring that their process meets their customer requirements.

Lean Production, the Theory of Constraints,[9] re-engineering, Six-Sigma and Total Quality Management all seek improvement by redefining work processes to eliminate the causes of variation and reduce waste, friction, cycle-time and costs in the process. I fear that with the packaging and selling of these programs, managers have come to see them as different things. They are not different things. You have one core work process. If you apply lean thinking, re-engineering, the Theory of Constraints, and continuously improve the process with Six-Sigma or TQM, you will be doing the same things, with slight differences in approach or language. Don't worry about the theories. Just improve the flow.

Process thinking becomes a way of life. Process thinking is learning to look horizontally through the organization as work flows. Those who are trained in lean processes can walk through a work setting and immediately see piles that signify process delays, interruptions in the form of pallets or in-boxes on the desk, or hear questions about "who owns the problem," all of which indicate

---

[9] Goldratt, Eliyahu M. *The Goal*, Great Barrington, MA: North River Press, 1984.

process problems. You should work on developing your automatic, habitual thoughts about process. Developing this competence will serve you well.

THE ATTITUDES OF PROCESS IMPROVEMENT:

- Most problems are in the process, not the person!
- Don't blame the person - fix the process.
- Every process can be improved – forever!
- Problems are normal – each an opportunity to learn.
- Measurement of processes leads to improvement.
- Every process must have a "process owner" or team responsible for its execution and improvement.
- We "know what we are doing" by knowing the process.

DIFFERENT TYPES OF PROCESSES MAPS

A process is a set of related activities that together result in a desired output for a customer. That set of activities can simply be listed on a sheet of paper. However, we have all heard the saying that a picture is worth a thousand words. It is true. If you have ever downloaded directions on Mapquest, you received a list of turns and highways. You then also see the map of the suggested route. The map is much more helpful. Human beings were created as visual creatures. We like to see pictures, and we find it easier to understand a picture than a list of words.

You will have to decide the most useful way to map your process. It will be helpful to look at a number of different process maps and see how each may be useful in different situations.

MACRO MAPS

Let's start with a very high level map. Think of "macro maps" as looking at your organization from an airplane thirty thousand feet in the air. They give you the big picture.

The first map is a "Strategy Map." This describes a process of moving an organization toward a strategy to better serve its customers. It is a bit complex, but that is because it involves a very big issue with lots of parts. This is a map that might be helpful to the most senior managers, but not very helpful to teams at the first level.

It includes both the external perspective of the marketplace and the internal perspective of what we do to achieve our strategic goals. It starts by defining the business strategy – where do we want to be positioned in the marketplace and what will create shareholder value. It looks at what is important to the customer and how we create "brand equity" that then results in shareholder value. It also includes a definition of principles that are important to our company. The ones given are just examples. It then looks at

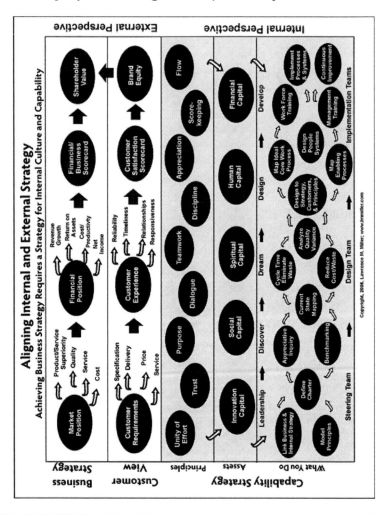

the assets, not only financial, but all forms of capital, including social (trust), spiritual (purpose and value), and human (competencies and motivation). Finally, it maps the "what do we do?" of a change process and who will do it. Developing this kind of a strategy map is a very useful exercise for senior managers so that they can understand the relationship between business results and a change process.

The following is another high level map. This is a macro map of a business process for an entire company. Every senior management team should develop a macro map of its business process. A senior manager should be responsible for each of the major components of the core work process (R&D, product, marketing, sales & service) and each of the major enabling processes. Often, the senior management team is made up of the individuals who head each of these areas.

Macro Business System

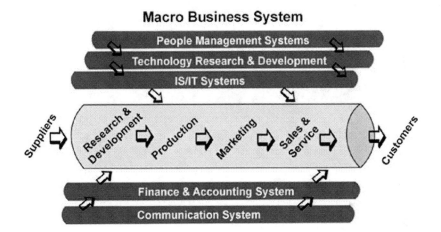

WORK PROCESS MAPS

Your team is more likely to be concerned with a more detailed description of how you do your daily work. A map that describes the work we do is a work process map. Again, there are many different ways to map work processes, so it will help to look at a few examples.

The following is a very simple map created by a team responsible for managing a conference. You will see that they have identified the major core activities across the top. This was their first map of their process. Then, they decided that more detail would be needed so they "drilled down" and mapped the detailed steps within each of the original general steps. You can see that under "define customers, needs and goals" they have mapped the five steps for getting that job done. Of course, they did this for each of the seven steps.

One of the advantages of doing this is that this team plans and manages a conference each year. In the past, every time they had to plan a conference, they would have new members who had not done it before. So the learning would begin again with little or no memory of the lessons of previous years. Now, at the beginning of their planning for the conference they take out the planning map and review the steps from last year. They decided whether these steps still make sense this year, and they assign responsibility for each of the steps. Then, after that conference is completed, they have a learning-reflection meeting. They review what went well and what did not go well. They look at the map again and make

Conference Planning Process

Appoint Conference Committee → Define Customers, Needs, Goals → Develop Agenda, Presenters → Develop Marketing Plan → Implement Marketing → Conduct Conference → Review Feedback Evaluate

Define Customers, Needs, Goals ↓
Review Last Year's Feedback ↓
Define Desired and Past Customers ↓
Benchmark Other Conferences ↓
Survey Sample Customers ↓
Reach Consensus on Needs & Goals

changes so the team next year can avoid any mistake they made. In this way, each annual team is able to improve the process and maintain some "corporate memory." This is a form of knowledge management that is often lacking in organizations.

IDENTIFYING THE "VALUE" IN THE PROCESS STREAM

Another name for process mapping is value stream mapping. What is the meaning of "value?" Value is created when there is a transformation in the material, information, or other input, and that transformation is necessary to satisfy the customer who will pay for every step in this process. Anything that does not add value is waste. Sitting still is waste. Re-doing is waste. Any time spent that is not directly creating the desired transformations is waste. The job of the team studying a process is to identify exactly which

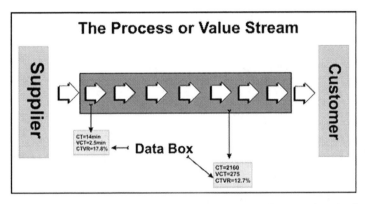

time, materials, motions, etc., are adding value and which are waste.

Value adding and non-value adding activity can be identified on your process map by using data boxes. Below you will see an example. These data boxes illustrate three measures of value: CT, the actual cycle time from beginning to the end of that process step; VCT, the value adding cycle time; and CTVR the ratio of value adding to total cycle time.

Identifying the actual cycle time and the value adding time requires discipline, doing your homework. You should not guess. Go and see! Go and measure! Get the data. Often, it will surprise you.

Below you will see a completed analysis of cycle time for one process. The total and value-adding cycle time of each step has been identified, as well as the totals for the overall process. The percent of value adding time is 12.7%. This is not an unusual ratio when processes are studied carefully. You will see that this team has set an ambitious goal of getting to 50% value adding time. This will mean eliminating a lot of non-value adding activity, delays, re-do loops, or other interruptions in the process.

Which value measures you decide to use when analyzing your process will be dependent on the nature of the work and the output of the work. Beginning with cycle time, analysis is one of the most certain ways to get started.

Common Process or Value Measures

- CT = Cycle Time
- VCT=Value Adding Cycle Time
- CTVR=Ratio of Value Adding to Total Cycle Time
- CO=Change Over Time
- No.O=Number of Separate Operations
- WT=Work Time (actual value adding work)
- TT=Total Time Worked or Assigned to an Operation
- SC=Scrap
- SCR=Scrap rate (ratio of scrap to total)
- I=Inventory

BUT YOU decide what process measures are most important for your process!!!

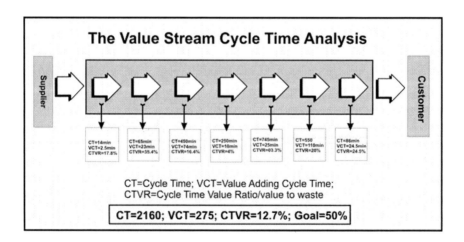

1.	Invite guests to dinner.
2.	Decide on the menu.
3.	Go shopping.
4.	Cut the onions and brown.
5.	Add and brown meat.
6.	Cut and add green pepper and mushrooms.
7.	Add tomato sauce.
8.	Add spices.
9.	Simmer for two hours.
10.	Make salad.
11.	Cook vegetable.
12.	Warm water to boil.
13.	Set table.
14.	Add spaghetti to water.
15.	Rinse spaghetti.
16.	Serve above.
17.	Eat.
18.	Clean table.
19.	Wash dishes.

This is a very simple map. This is a process with which we are all familiar. It is a simple work process: making a meal. If you are a good cook (like me!) you know that the order in which you do things is very important. For example, if you are going to make a spaghetti dinner, you don't start your preparations by sticking the pasta in a pot of cold water, and then thinking about how to prepare the sauce. You begin preparing the sauce long before putting water on to boil for the spaghetti. Order is important in most work processes. It is one of the reasons why you should map your processes. Problems often occur because the order is wrong. Or you have missed a step or have unnecessary steps.

While this process map is useful, it is also lacking a lot of very helpful information. Who is doing what? Why is one person doing something and not other people? Does one person bear too much responsibility or not enough?

It is much easier to find answers to these questions in a "relationship map." The following map contains exactly the same steps; it is the same process, as the previous one. But, now you have who is doing what. You can see that Dad is doing the majority of the work. Maybe he wants it this way, or maybe he doesn't, but it

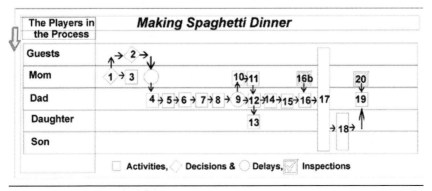

certainly raises some questions that should be asked. You can see that relationship problems are often created by how we do things, the relationships reflected in the process. What problems do you think this process might lead to? You might try reversing the roles of Mom and Dad. Do you like it better or worse that way? Why?

DESIGN YOUR PROCESS TO PRINCIPLES:

You can't claim to be principle-centered if your processes do not conform to your principles. Your processes are what you do, not what you say.

If you say that you believe in "decision-making at the lowest possible level," for example, look at your process and ask whether it conforms to this principle. If you say you believe in continuous improvement, are your processes designed to incorporate the mechanisms of continuous improvement?

Almost every company has developed a statement of values or principles that hangs on the walls of the company. Unfortunately, too often employees walk by and read it, then say to themselves, "Sounds great, I wish I worked there!" Many employees become skeptical and de-motivated by witnessing behavior and processes that contradict the stated values. Involve them in analyzing those processes and assessing their conformance to principles. To the degree that they are involved in this analysis and work toward align process to principles; they will have respect for their company and its management.

KNOCK THE WALLS DOWN – INTERRUPTION FREE WINS!

Customers don't care about your walls. If you buy a computer or television from Best Buys, it either works or it doesn't. If it doesn't, you are unhappy with Best Buys, not HP who may have their label on the computer, although they probably didn't manufacture it. And the problem may be one chip or hard drive in the computer that wasn't manufactured by the company that assembled the computer. But the customer doesn't care about any of that. Next time, he will shop somewhere else.

Customers look horizontally through a process. It is all one flow to them, and the customer is always right. Do you remember our patient who died trying to jump over walls and hurdles in the health care system, all the system of one company? Banging into walls killed her. It is our responsibility to create a "seamless" or "boundary-less" process flow. Interruptions cost money, increase inventory costs, increase the cost of quality, slow cycle times, and result in poor service. Interrupted processes are killing companies.

One way to address this is to "flow" through the process personally and "be" the thing being made. It may sound a bit silly, but try it, and you will be amazed. Pretend that you are incoming material supply. Get off the truck. Go to the warehouse. Sit on a shelf. How do you like it so far? How long do you sit there? When you go to the next stop (notice the word "stop") in the process, how long do you sit (interruption) there? How often are you recycled? It is probably very frustrating. As you walk through this process, have a pad of paper and pencil handy. Write down every possible improvement, every possible elimination of a wall or interruption. Now ask yourself, if I were this thing, how would I like to be treated? What would I like the process to be in order to help me become the best end-product I can become in the shortest period of time?

The worst walls and interruptions in most processes, are jumping over the legal walls between companies. Customers don't care about companies. The first criterion in selecting a supplier should be whether they are willing to work with you in a seamless, interruption free manner. Are they willing to serve on a team that designs the process? Are they willing to work with you to minimize in-process inventory? Are they willing to respond to quality issues within hours, not days, weeks or months? Are they willing to share financial and quality data in a completely transparent manner? These are the issues that create competitive advantage and result in lower total costs.

HOW TO TURN PROCESSES INTO FLOW

Here are some simple steps to follow to create a process map.

1. CLARIFY PURPOSE AND GOALS

The purpose and goals of every process should be clear. You have may have already done this. Just review them here. The purpose should make clear why the process is important and to whom. The goals should not be detailed scorecard goals, but the general goal of the process.

2. AGREE ON RESPONSIBILITY

Is the process the responsibility of the entire team, more than one team, or just a few members of the team? The process should be defined by those who "own" the process. Who owns this process?

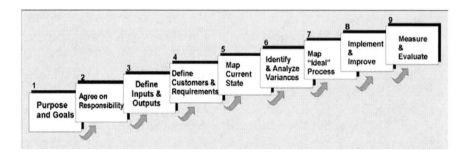

3. DEFINE INPUTS & OUTPUTS

If you have completed the work in the previous chapters, you have already done much the necessary work to be ready to work on process improvement. You should have answers to the following questions

- What are the inputs to your work process (include materials, information, capital, people)? What are the requirements for each of these inputs?

- Who are the suppliers who provide input? What capabilities are needed on the part of suppliers in order to meet these requirements?

- What are the feedback loops from your team to your suppliers, and how do they function (speed, quality of information)?
- What are the outputs of your work system?
- Given the above, what are the requirements for your work process?
- What are the feedback loops that inform us of customer satisfaction, and how do they function (speed, quality of information)?

4. DEFINE CUSTOMER REQUIREMENT

If you followed the guidance in the previous chapters, you have this. It is helpful to just put this on a flip chart so the team can see and refer to these requirements as they begin mapping the process.

5. MAP THE CURRENT STATE

It is a mistake to start mapping how you think things should be until you have mapped how things actually get done today. This is the "current state" of the process.

It is often true that even people doing the job don't know how the whole process gets done. People only understand their very narrow piece of the work. You can't analyze how things can be improved or study the causes of variances if you don't know how things are currently done. First, map the current state of the process.

It may be helpful to imagine a meeting in which a team is going to map their process. Let's go through how that meeting might flow:

a. First, let's check to see that we have the right people in the room. Are the team members in this room the "world's greatest experts" in this process? Is there anyone else we should invite to participate in mapping the process?

b. Now let's define the process. Do we agree on the process boundaries? Where does this process begin and where does it end?

c. Now we will make a list of the inputs and outputs and customer requirements for this process. We will also make a list of any other specifications for the output of this process.

d. Now let's map the current state steps in the process. Let's start this by brainstorming without worrying about whether we have the steps in exactly the right order. It is very helpful to have Post-It-Notes, especially the 3x5 kind. Have the team members write down steps in the process and put those on the wall. It is very helpful to have a roll of brown paper that you can spread across the wall. Give yourself lots of room.

e. Some process steps are work activities; some are decisions. If you can, use a different color for these. Or you can indicate in some way that these are symbols. Agree on another kind of note for delays.

f. Give everyone a chance to get all of the steps up on the wall and then ask, "Who are the Players in the process?" Make a note for each individual who participates in the work of this process. Now put these players in a vertical column to the left of your paper. If you can, draw a horizontal line across the paper, representing the occasions when that player may be involved.

g. Now order the steps. Arrange each of the work steps and decisions on your map going from left to right. They should be in chronological order. If two things are happening at the same time, they can be on top of each other. If they happen after one another, then they should be to the right of the previous step.

h. Ask yourself how these happen in time. Are there delays between steps? If these delays are for any significant amount of time, put a post-it-note up for that delay.

i. Now create a timeline from left to right. It may be that the process is not the same every time. Take a typical process cycle for the sake of your studying the process. On the left, when the process begins, put a zero at the beginning of your timeline. Then, at the end of the process put the amount of time a typical cycle takes, whether it is one hour or one month. Then, try to put time marks from left to right as the steps occur. This will give you some idea where the delays are occurring and how much time is involved in each step of the process. This may raise some questions when you analyze the process for speed or cycle time improvement.

j. This is probably enough work for one meeting. Getting to this point may have taken one to several hours. When a team is assigned to work on a complex process that flows through the organization, just mapping the current state may involve many meetings over a period of weeks. It may also be necessary to go and interview other people who are working in the process in order to have knowledge of those steps.

k. It is sometimes desirable at this point to invite others into the meeting, perhaps some managers, perhaps members of other teams and ask them if they agree that this is how things currently work. They may have some insights that your team may have missed.

l. It will probably be in another meeting that you begin to analyze the variances in the process. Below is an introduction to the analysis of variances. This will be explored in more detail in the following chapter.

6. Identify and Analyze Variances:

A variance is anything in a process that varies from the way things should ideally be done or a result that varies from customer requirements. The next chapter will deal in more depth with analyzing variances.

7. Map the "Ideal" Process

There is no such thing as an ideal process. There is only the most ideal process we can imagine at this time. That ideal will change as we experiment and learn more about our process. But for now, map what you regard to be the ideal process. Start where input comes into the organization and the first step is taken. Go through all the steps you would recommend for a future process.

Be sure not to add back in waste or sources of variance that you have eliminated.

8. IMPLEMENT AND IMPROVE

If you have followed all of the steps above, it is now time to implement your new and improved process. However, you may feel that you have more work to do to analyze problems in the process. If this is the case, the next couple of chapters will help you find and make those improvements. Finding improvement and implementing those improvements should be an ongoing process, something you do many times in a year. By finding and implementing improvements to your process, you are doing your job as a high performance team.

9. MEASURE AND EVALUATE

If you have developed your team scorecard, you have identified measures of your work process. These are measures that you should be graphing and monitoring on a daily or weekly basis. The improvements you have made in your process should be reflected in these scores.

CHAPTER *13*

Analyzing Variances in Performance

There is statistical variation and there is a variance from how things could ideally be done. Both are problems within a process, and both need to be the focus of attention by your team.

Statistical variation is the variability around a mean for any performance. For example, you may have a gun that you aim at a target. Let's assume that you are one hundred yards away from that target. Let's also assume that there is no wind and the gun is in a vice-grip so it will not move. Will every bullet land in exactly the same spot, assuming that the gun itself is perfectly stable? They will not all fall in the same place. If you fire fifty shots from the gun, you will see a pattern. That pattern can be described as statistical variation, the variability around a mean. The average bullet may fall at or very close to the target, but the pattern will be in a circle around that point. Depending on the gun, the pattern may be a few inches wide or a few feet. This pattern will describe the capability of this system in its current state.

COMMON AND SPECIAL CAUSES OF VARIATION

Dr. Deming described the important distinction between what he called *common cause* and *special cause* of variation. In the example of the bullets hitting a target, if you fire fifty or one hundred shots, you will see that all of the shots fall within some circle. This variation from the mean, the center of the circle, is *common cause*. In other words, it is inherent in the nature of the system. The gun is a system with inputs, a process, and an output. The variability, under stable conditions (the gun is clean, it is not moving, etc.) that results from this system is common cause. Within the normal performance of this system, the only explanation for each variation is simple randomness. There is always random variability around a mean. Every system produces variation that describes the capability of that system. You can and should expect it. If you want to reduce this variation, reduce the size of the circle made by the bullets, you will have to change the nature of the system. You could add a longer barrel on the gun and that would probably reduce the variation.

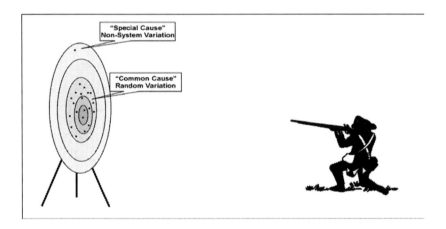

But, there is another kind of variation and this is not the result of the inherent properties of the system. A *special cause* is the result of something "being wrong" in the operation of the system. In other words, if the circle on the target is normally a radius of twelve inches, this is "system" performance. However, if suddenly a bullet falls two feet away from the center, you know that this is not normal for this system. You only know this because you already have data on system performance. You immediately say "Hey, something is wrong here!" And what you mean is that "Hey, this is not a common cause; this is a special cause of variation." This is caused by some abnormality in the system or abnormal input. Now you can brainstorm the possible causes of this defect. The cause may be a bad bullet. Or something may have knocked and moved the gun. The gun may be getting dirty. There may be many possible reasons for a special cause.

The important point of this distinction is that you will do different things depending on whether the variation is a special or common cause variation. If you seek to improve the normal variation produced by a system, common cause, you will have to redesign that system. On the other hand, if you are witnessing a special cause, you would be making a serious mistake to redesign the system. This would cause even more variation. You need to track down the reason you have experienced a special cause.

THE COST OF VARIATION

There is a cost to variation. For example, when you drive to work each day it may take an average of thirty minutes to make the drive from home to work. But, it is rarely exactly thirty minutes. It may vary ten minutes on either side. If the weather and traffic are good, you may get to work in twenty minutes. But if there is an accident, it could take a lot more than thirty minutes. Let us assume that you live in an area where there is a lot of road construction and there tend to be a lot of accidents. When there is no traffic and no construction, the process of driving from home to work is

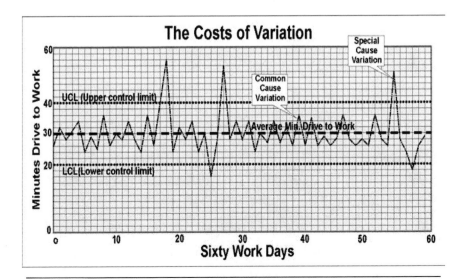

"interruption free." But, in your situation, during a normal drive to work hours, there is a fair likelihood of an interruption, something that will cause a deviation from the mean.

Now let's also assume that there are some consequences for being either late or early. Your team cannot start work until you get there. If one person is late by thirty minutes, that is the equivalent of all ten members of the team being late. The consequence is that there are three hundred minutes of lost work time. Being on time is so important that it is a factor in your performance reviews. If you are late too many times, that may result in not achieving a merit increase in pay. This is a risk that you do not want to take. On the other hand, if you are thirty minutes early, the door is locked and you can't enter. This means standing out in the cold. These are the costs of variation in the process. Variation almost always has costs even if we fail to see or understand them. We often behave on the assumption of variability in a process and we therefore consider it "just the way things are."

If you look at the above graph, you can see this variation illustrated. You have measured the time it takes you to drive to work for sixty days. The average is thirty minutes, but on three occasions it took about fifty minutes. On two occasions it took less than twenty minutes. Now that you know about the consequences of extreme variation (defining extreme as above or below the control limits), would you alter your behavior? What are the costs associated with this variation?

VARIATION IN HUMAN PERFORMANCE

The examples given above are oriented to the manufacturing setting. In knowledge work, the rate and process of work is much more independently controlled by the individual. For example, if you are creating advertising, you cannot define exactly how each creative process is going to proceed as if it was a repetitive process such as one on an assembly line. It may be that the best creative work may be watching television or taking a walk around the block to get ideas. If you are writing grant proposals, each proposal will require some different information and will require unique research and writing. When one understands the actual work involved, one is in a better position to judge the nature of the variation.

Variation is often a result of interaction with the uncontrollable events in the environment. Imagine a football team. Even if the team played the same opponent with the same players every game, there would still be some variation in performance. The quarterback would not throw the same number of completed passes each game. But in the real world, every opponent is different, with different defensive schemes, and this will cause variation in the play of the quarterback. You can think of the job of the defense as doing everything they can to create variances in the play of the quarterback.

Much of our work is like this, continually adjusting to the customer, the economic conditions, and competitors. The trick is to learn what forces are influencing performance, seek to control those we can control, and adjust to those we cannot control.

Selling is also a human performance process that is very much under the control of the individual, but also continually interacts with forces in the environment. How does the idea of variation apply to these types of human performance?

In the chart below you will see the annual performance for a team of new car salesman in a group of auto dealerships. This is a "cumulative" graph. That means that each data point is added to

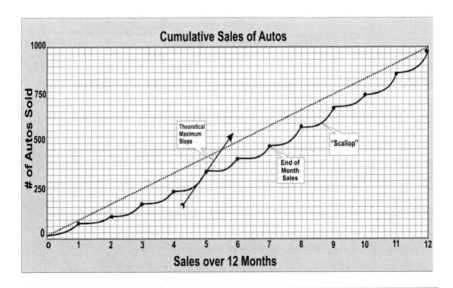

the previous data points, so it never goes down. You will see that for the year the sales team will sell approximately one thousand automobiles. That does not mean that each month they will sell exactly one twelfth of this number. If they sold exactly the same amount each month, all end–of–month sales points would be on the line that is on the slope from zero to one thousand. You will also notice that within each month there is a pattern. Sales vary from the first week of the month to the last week. In fact, in every case, the last week of the month has much stronger sales than the first week of the month. If you were the manager of this organization, it would probably benefit you to know why there is this variation in performance. What do you think is causing this end of month increase in sales?

You will also notice that if you take the maximum slope that occurs during the last week of the month and project this line, it is a significantly greater rate of performance than the average performance for the year.

The curve of performance within each month is what is known as a *scallop.* It is very familiar to experimental psychologists who study the science of human behavior, particularly what are called *schedules of reinforcement.* The sales people in this organization are very clearly on what is called a fixed-interval schedule of reinforcement. What this simply means is the rewards are delivered at the end of each month. After the end of each month, these salespeople experience what is known as a *post-reinforcement-pause.* These sales people receive a monthly bonus check for their sales during the previous month. They receive this on the first day of the month. They do what most people do: as the potential reward approaches, they work harder to get that reward. We have all done this. It is the same as cramming the night before for the test in school. Congress passes the largest number of bills just before they achieve the reward of going home at the end of the session.

If you are a customer, what does this tell you about when is the best time to buy a car? When are you likely to get the best deal? It will be during the last few days of the month, of course. The incentive system conditions the sales people, and the sales people condition the customers to buy at the end of the month.

Understanding this pattern of variability and its cause can be extremely valuable to the organization. How could the reward system be modified to reduce the variability and increase the total sales? The answer is in shifting from a fixed-interval (once a month on the last day of the month) reward schedule, to one that varies and has the element of surprise, like all gambling that maintains strong and consistent rates of behavior.

There are many costs to variability in sales. Inventories are often determined by the maximum demand on inventory. In other words, the salesman will want to have on-site enough cars and sufficient variety to meet their customers' needs during that last days of the month. But this elevates the inventory level to one that is unnecessary for three weeks out of the month. There is also the cost of offering excessively "good deals" during the last week when the sales people are frantic to bring in every possible sale. These patterns of performance are entirely based on human behavior and have nothing to do with anything mechanical.

CHAPTER *14*

FINDING AND ELIMINATING WASTE

For more than forty years, Toyota has worked to improve the process of designing and building cars by focusing on the elimination of waste. They are still doing it today. For how long have you been eliminating waste from your processes?

Contrary to the understanding of many, the primary focus of improvement in lean organizations has not been making more money or managing quality, although both have been the result. The primary driver for improvement has been the elimination of waste. It is not the same as cost reduction!

Most companies cut costs, usually meaning cut people, and leave the waste. The waste is in the process, not the person. If you eliminate the waste in the process, you can then redeploy the person and other assets to "value-adding" work and thereby increase value to customers. That is how you make money. Company after company has gone out of business cutting costs, which results in worse products, worse service, fearful employees who lose their creativity, and the inevitable loss of customers. You stay in business by maximizing value to customers.

Lean teaching generally focuses on the elimination of the seven forms of waste identified by Shigeo Shingo at Toyota. We will get to those. But, since this is a Leader's Guide, let's start the discussion of waste where it may be closer to home. Let's start with waste that occurs in the management ranks.

ELIMINATE MANAGEMENT WASTE

The new challenge for lean management is to improve the efficiency of management itself. Much management activity is waste. This waste is just as destructive, or more so, than waste on the factory floor.

What does this waste look like? I have identified six forms of management waste.

MANAGEMENT WASTE # 1: SUCKING DECISIONS UP DUE TO THE LACK OF EMPOWERMENT, EDUCATION AND ENCOURAGEMENT AT LOWER LEVELS.

Management thinks they are busy because they are doing other people's work and they do this because they have not structured the organization, established the training and systems to create competent problem-solving and decisions at lower levels. They waste time meddling in the work of others.

MANAGEMENT WASTE #2: DISPLAYING CONTRADICTORY MODELS.

If you want to teach your children not to smoke, drink or swear, but you walk around the house smoking, drinking and swearing, your efforts are going to be little more than waste. Management, leaders, must model the behavior they desire of others. The failure to do so cripples any change effort. Millions of dollars in consulting and training have become waste because management didn't walk the talk.

MANAGEMENT WASTE #3: FAILURE TO DEFINE AND MANAGE YOUR OWN PROCESSES.

There are processes that are owned by the senior management team. Every team, at every level, should have a SIPOC that defines input, output, and value adding processes owned by that team. They don't own any process? Than the entire team is waste! Tell them to go home. Most management teams do not know what there processes are, and reinvent them in a random or annual manner.

Developing strategy is a senior management value-adding process. Where is the map that visualizes how they develop strategy? When they did it last year, did they study the process and what did they learn? Unfortunately, they probably learned nothing and are not themselves engaged in continuous improvement. Therefore, they don't understand it and do not set the model.

MANAGEMENT WASTE #4: FAILURE OF DECISION-MAKING:

I have coached dozens of senior management teams. One would think, logically, that the higher you go in the company, the more skilled would be the decision makers and decision-making process. The value of decisions made at the top, should be of greatest value. Errors made at the top are the most expensive. The truth is that in most companies, the decision-making process at the top is terrible.

Many years ago I was doing a socio-tech redesign of a major financial organization on Wall Street. The only room the design team could find to meet in was THE BOARD ROOM!! Very expensive furniture, huge table, mahogany paneled walls, etc. After a day or two the design team had half the wall area covered with flip chart sheets. In stormed the official keeper of the room with steam spurting out of his ears. He yelled, "Take that down immediately! No one has ever put anything on these walls!" I asked, "Really? No one has ever brainstormed or put flip charts on the walls in here?" "Absolutely Not!" He yelled back. Poor fellow. He had never seen a room in which people were actually solving problems, brainstorming, reaching consensus, developing action plans, etc. It tells you a lot about how senior management teams fail to employ disciplined decision processes.

MANAGEMENT WASTE #5: WASTED SPACE AND RESOURCES.

That board room was used once a quarter. It sat empty and unused most of the time. Why do managers need larger offices as they move up the ladder? Do they get fatter? Do they have bigger computers or more books? What is that about? It is about waste. It is the waste of ego. The time spent at resorts doing annual strategic planning that could be done in their own conference room, or in someone's home, is also waste. Apply the same disciplined standards of waste and resource utilization at the executive and management level as you apply to the factory floor.

MANAGEMENT WASTE #6: THE FAILURE OF TRUST.

An effective management team, like any team, is a social system built on trust. That trust enables members to share, to ask questions, to offer suggestions, and to listen well to each other. On most management teams there is a failure of trust among its members that inhibits their ability to solve problems and make effective decisions.

The solution to these forms of waste, which is the opposite of lean management, is not only training, but coaching and feedback. They need hands on help in order to change their behavior, their habits. It is these habits that define the culture.

THE TRADITIONAL SEVEN FORMS OF WASTE

Any activity that does not directly contribute to producing the product or service is waste. Warehouses do not directly contribute to productive work. Pallets, bins, empty space, any area where re-work is done, people who do re-work, unnecessary supervision, control and management are all waste. The more of these you can eliminate while maintaining the speed and quality of the process, the better. Many of these forms of waste slow down the process and even create quality problems. And do not think these are only in manufacturing. They are just more visible in manufacturing. In office environments they are more hidden in reports re-written, decisions re-made, delays in decisions, and papers sitting in inboxes waiting for a response. You just can't see them "out on the floor", but they are just as costly.

The founders of Lean Manufacturing were Taichi Ohno and Dr. Shigeo Shingo. They focused on seven types of waste:

1. **Inventory:** Any "piles" are waste. Anything that is standing still and not in motion is waste, whether it is in a warehouse or in bins or on pallets in the production area.

Inventory consumes space (waste), requires employees to move and manage (waste), inventory requires accounting (waste), and instead having one mistake that is caught immediately, you will have a large pile of defects... big waste! Just-in-time is the process of arranging the supply chain and production process so that each input arrives at the process just in time, and each output goes directly to the next stage of the process, just in time.

2. **Motion:** Motion is a key variable addressed by industrial engineering. Teams in lean processes constantly study their motions to determine how motions can be eliminated or made easier by adjusting equipment, benches, etc.

3. **Transportation:** If steps in the process are separated by physical space, forklifts, trucks, dollies, or other mechanisms of transportation are required. All of this is waste. The production process should be designed to minimize transportation.

4. **Defects:** Every defective product is waste. The time, effort, and supply that went into producing it are waste. Re-working errors is necessary, but waste, because if it had been done right the first time, the re-work would not be needed. It is the job of the team to use problem-solving methods to study and eliminate waste.

5. **Waiting time:** Kanban and other methods in lean production are designed to eliminate waiting time. People should be flexible, trained, and assigned to move from one job to another in a production area so they can smooth the flow of production elements to prevent waiting for someone else to do something that only he or she can do.

6. **Overproduction:** Overproduction produces the need for storage, big piles rather than small piles. At the beginning the lean production process was Shigeo Shingo's work on the die change process that resulted in Single Minute Exchange of Dies. Dies in a metal stamping process (common in auto production) must be changed for each part. In some operations in old style manufacturing it took an entire day to change dies, a separate die change crew, die change department, die change managers, etc. – all waste. Working with the press team and constantly asking them the right questions, he was able to show them how to

reduce die change down to single minutes, allowing for small lot production which, of course, eliminated many of the other sins of waiting time and inventory.

7. **Processing:** By processing Shingo is referring to inefficiencies within a process – things done the wrong way, lack of training, etc.

I know that many readers will say "What a minute, this is all about manufacturing, and I work in a service business. In fact, manufacturing is far more efficient and has done much more to eliminate waste than service and management functions. There is far more waste in management activity, accounting, selling, servicing, etc. How many times have you been told to hurry up and get a report written, and then the report sits in someone's inbox for a week before it is reviewed or put to use? Waste! Because you are a knowledge worker, think. Understand the philosophy, the mental process involved in lean organizations, and you will recognize that most of these forms of waste are present within your own work system.

My good friend Norman Bodek tells a Shingo story that may help us understand the attitude of eliminating waste in his excellent book Kaikaku.[10] Norman used to put on "Productivity" conferences at which I spoke for many years. These should have been called Lean conferences, but that term had not been invented yet. His conferences usually include talks by one of the masters of lean manufacturing and Quality Management, as well as lesser folks like me. Norman made trips to Japan and made it his mission to translate and bring to the United States the lessons from these innovators.

This story is from one of the trips to the U.S. he arranged for Dr. Shingo.

On Dr. Shingo's first visit to America I took him to a Dresser, Inc. manufacturing plant, where they were producing gasoline fuel dispensing systems. After first meeting the management team we

---

[10] Bodek, Norman. Kaikaku: The Power and Magic of Lean. PCS Press, Vancouver Washington, 2004.

walked around the plant floor with a small group of engineers and managers.

Dr. Shingo stopped in front of a punch press. He asked us all to look at the operation and to tell us the percentage of *value adding time*. He then took out his stopwatch to time the operation.

We watched two workers in front of the punch press bend down and pick up a large sheet of thin stainless steel from the left side of the press. They placed the steel into the bed of the press. Then they removed their hands to press buttons outside the press, which indicated that their hands were out and clear of the press. The large press came down and formed the metal into a side of a gasoline pump. Then the two workers reached into the press, removed the formed sheet and placed the formed sheet at the right side of the press.

Dr. Shingo asked, "What was the value adding percentage?"

One engineer said "100%; the workers never stopped working."

Another engineer said "75%," and another said "50%."

Dr. Shingo laughed and looked at his stop watch. "Only 12% of the time was the process adding value. Adding value is only when the dies are pressing against the metal to create a formed sheet. The rest of the time is waste."

Dr. Shingo then asked, "What can be done to increase the percent of value adding time?"

An engineer immediately said, "You can place a table over here and put the raw inventory sheets on top of the table. This would help the workers. They wouldn't need to bend down. They could just slide the sheets directly into the press."

Another engineer said, "We could install a leveler to automatically raise the sheet metal to keep it at a constant height, similar to what you might see in a cafeteria when you reach for a dinner plate."

A third engineer said, "We could put a spring into the back of the punch press to force the formed metal to leap forward after the stamping."

Dr. Shingo laughed and said, "Yes, you all know what to do, so do it!"

An important point to notice in this story is that Dr. Shingo did not TELL them anything to do. He merely asked the right questions and defined things as they really are. He knew waste when he saw it. This is the primary characteristics of managers in lean operations. They ask the right questions. They constantly seek to improve by eliminating waste. Also notice that Shingo never suggested that there was anything wrong with the workers or that they weren't working hard enough. He did not blame the person; he assumed the problem was in the process.

The concept of "value-adding" is important. It is the activity and time that actually adds value to the end use customer. The customer doesn't care how many motions the workers go through, how much they have to moved stuff, store stuff, or rework stuff. That all just adds cost. If your manger told you to go run around the building five times, you might do it. You might get paid during that time, and you might call it "work." But what value did it add for the customer? None!

SEARCH FOR WASTE IN YOUR PROCESS:

Take a look at the following diagram. Where is the waste in this process? Look at each of the seven sins of waste that Ohno and Shingo described above. How many of them can you find in your process?

Now put your process on the wall. This time you should be certain to include all the delays, storage, waiting, etc. Now ask yourself: What is the actual amount of value adding time? What is

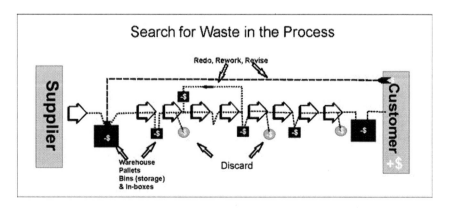

the total time from beginning to end? And what percentage is the value adding time?

CHAPTER *15*

A Disciplined Method of Problem-Solving

At the heart of the work of every team is solving problems to improve their process and performance. This book presents several problem-solving methodologies. Chapters 11-15 each present a different problem-solving or performance improvement approach. They are all useful. This chapter presents a comprehensive and disciplined approach to solving problems. Once you are familiar with these you can decide which is most appropriate for a given problem or performance.

It is useful to consider the philosophy of problem-solving. Many organizations are crippled by the wrong philosophy, and no methods will overcome the wrong philosophy.

A PHILOSOPHY OF PROBLEM-SOLVING

PROBLEMS ARE NORMAL!

You should solve problems every day. Solving problems is our job. It is why we come to work. If we had no problems, we would be terrifically bored. Celebrate problems! Every problem is an opportunity for learning.

Unfortunately, in the "old culture" before lean and TQM, it was common for managers to punish those who presented problems. They thought you were doing your job if you had no problems and brought no problems to them. I suppose they wanted to sit back at their desk, with their feet up in the air and proclaim that everything was running just fine. If you brought them problems, that disturbed their peace of mind. Of course, the problems didn't go away; they just became worse. In some cases they became accepted practice, just "the way we do things." The real problem was not solving problems every day.

When Dr. Deming said that we should drive out fear, he was addressing this philosophy. When you punish someone for pointing out a problem, you are creating fear. Fear hides problems, but it does not solve them.

THE PROBLEM IS THE PROCESS, NOT THE PERSON

Most problems can be solved by examining how we do things, the work process. Of course, sometimes they are the result of individuals not being adequately trained or informed. But, this lack of training or lack of information is, itself, a process problem. If you blame individuals for problems, you will again create fear and cause them to hide those problems. It is far better to say "I am sure you wanted to get a better result; let's see what caused the problem." By analyzing the problem, rather than blaming the person, you will find it much easier to make progress.

FAST IS GOOD AND QUICKER IS BETTER

Every problem has a cost that occurs in time. By not solving a problem now, you are spending money. If a problem is causing anxiety for a customer, with every passing day the probability increases that the customer will find another supplier. These costs are usually invisible because customers rarely tell you why they chose to buy a competitor's product or service. They generally do not consider that their responsibility. So it is your responsibility to find problems and solve them quickly.

THERE ARE NO PERFECT SOLUTIONS

Every day of our life is an experiment. We experiment with new items on the menu of a restaurant. We experiment with a new variety of soup when we go to the supermarket. We experiment with a new traffic route, a new television program, or a new website. We are constantly experimenting. This is how we learn.

In our daily life we recognize that we will never find the one right and final website that we will go to, or the final menu item, or the one right food in the grocery store. Why do we think we will find the perfect and final solution to any problem at work?

When we are solving problems, we are only finding the best solution we can find NOW with the facts and information we currently have. A week or month from now we will have new facts or information that may make a different solution seem better. Accepting this reality makes it that much easier to get on with the experimentation of implementing solutions. Every solution is a learning opportunity.

ADDRESS PROBLEMS THAT YOUR TEAM CAN CONTROL

It is always more fun to find problems that someone else should fix. It is why we enjoy sports or politics. We think politicians should fix everything, and we enjoy pointing out what a terrible job they are doing. This is fun because we are spectators.

You may remember the prisoners who blame the "other guy" for every bad thing that happened in their life. This "external locus-of-control" results in never taking responsibility for the events in their lives, never solving problems, and therefore, never learning. Don't be a team of "other guy" blamers. It will get you nowhere. Focus on the problems that you can solve. It will be much more rewarding.

TRUST IN THE POWER OF COLLECTIVE INTELLIGENCE

Let us assume that you are the smartest person on your team. It may even be true. But your knowledge and intelligence is only a fraction of the combined knowledge and intelligence of the team. Just imagine if you could somehow lift out of each brain their experience, wisdom, and intelligence and put it in a pile in the middle of a table. Now put your brainpower on the table next to it. Your brainpower will be small in comparison.

The magic of effective group problem-solving is that the collective brain power of the group expands to the degree that it combines. In other words, if you and I have an open conversation about a problem, it is likely that there will emerge from our "thinking together," rather than alone, a solution which will be something that neither of us would have arrived at on our own. We are now both smarter than when we began the conversation. So when we add our knowledge and experience together, that group brain pile is not merely the sum of our brainpower when we began. It doubles.

There is no way that your individual brainpower can match the collective intelligence of the group... if the group is able to create collective intelligence.

Think about how problems are solved in your team. How is the above philosophy of problem-solving practiced, or not? What would you do differently if you adopted this philosophy?

I WANT THE FACTS, NOTHING BUT THE FACTS!

Many years ago, before most readers of this book were born, there was a television detective show, probably the first "cops and robbers" show called *Dragnet*. Sergeant Friday was the central character. In each show he would interview some witness to a crime, and he would always say "I just want the facts, nothing but the facts."

It is easy to form opinions. The moment someone walks into the room, we form an opinion of them. But we don't know them. We don't know the facts. We don't know what happened at home this morning; we don't know what pain they are suffering; we don't know what they can contribute. Opinions without facts are easy. But effective problem-solving is always based on a period of gathering the facts. Too often we think we know the facts when we only know some small portion of the facts. Someone else has other portions, other facts. Let's play Sergeant Friday... first, nothing but the facts.

ADOPT A DISCIPLINED MODEL OF PROBLEM-SOLVING

For many years, even before the quality movement, there were many models of problem-solving. Many writers have defined the five, six, or seven steps to problem-solving. Most of these models include the same or very similar elements. There is no one right model or one best way. What is a best way is to adopt a disciplined process and follow it. It is not so important which one.

When the TQM process was the primary model, the PDCA (Plan, Do, Check and Act) model of problem-solving was very popular. This is obviously very simple and easy to follow.

With the promotion of Six-Sigma, a more

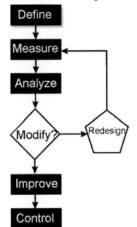

thorough model has been used in hundreds of companies with great success. This is the DMAIC Methodology.

Define, Measure, Analyze, Improve, and Control are the steps in this methodology.

This author prefers the following model simply because it is a bit more explicit and includes some elements that I believe are important and left out of either of the two previous models. This model can be summarized (and you can even pronounce it easier than DMAIC!) by the acronym DIMPABAC:

- **Define** the problem to be solved;
- **Inquire** with all those who have facts regarding the problem to gain different understanding and insight;
- **Measure** actual performance on the problem;
- **Principles** should be defined that are important to understanding this problem and its solution;
- **Analyze** the data on the causes of the problem;
- **Brainstorm** solutions to the problem;
- **Agree** to **Act** on a solution;
- **Control** the performance, and evaluate results.

In the following section of this chapter, we will discuss some of the possible ways you may go about each of these steps. However, this should be regarded as merely an introduction. There are many useful tools that are not discussed, primarily because it would require an entire book, itself, and because there are numerous other books or manuals available that do a good job of describing these tools.

1. DEFINE THE PROBLEM

What makes for a good problem definition? Imagine that you are not feeling well and you go to your doctor's office. Now let's imagine that there are three doctors there. Immediately after you walk into the office the three doctors stare at you at the same time. One doctor looks at you and says "Darn, he really looks sick." The second doctor looks at you and says "I don't see it. He looks fine to me." And, the third doctor says, "Well exactly where does it hurt and how long has it felt that way? Let's take some tests and measure a few of your vital signs and then let's make a judgment."

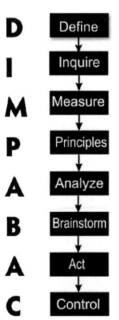

In which of these doctors do you have the most confidence? I think it would be the third one. Why? Because, the first two doctors are telling you how they feel, rather than how you feel, based on little information. Their judgments have as much to do with them as they do with you. The judgment that you look "really sick" is pretty useless. It is a very inadequate problem definition. Every doctor knows that you cannot begin to prescribe a remedy until you have a good definition of the problem – where it hurts, how long it has hurt, exactly where the pain is, etc. Similarly, your problem definition should be specific and it should be based on hard data.

A good problem definition has what is called "inter-observer reliability." This is a fancy way of saying that if three or four people see the same thing, they will be able to reach the same conclusion. The description will allow all of them to know it when they see it. For example, if you are describing a problem of a hitter in baseball, you might say that he is a "weak hitter." This may be true, but there is likely no inter-observer reliability. Two observers could easily get into an argument as to whether this player is a "weak" hitter. On the other hand, if you say that this hitter has an on-base percentage of .165, assuming your facts are correct, this is hard to argue with. Two people looking at the facts would agree on this definition of the problem. The problem to be solved is "how to increase his on-base percentage." That definition is a measure of performance.

You could also describe the problem in terms of *pinpointed behavior*. You could describe how this player is slow to get the bat off his shoulder and is late to swing 50% of the time. Two observers, if they were trained and observed carefully, would likely come up with the same definition of the problem or be able to recognize the problem you have described.

These more specific definitions are far more helpful in leading us to a solution than simply to say that this ball player is a "weak" hitter.

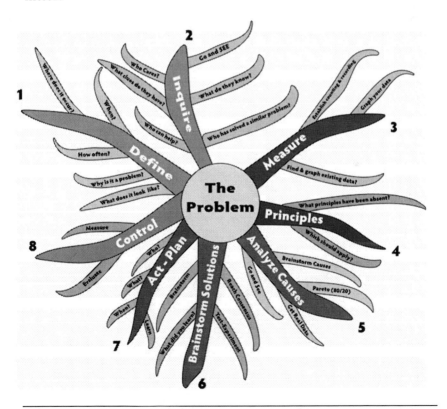

2. INQUIRE

Sometimes when you begin to solve a problem, you will have all the experts and information in the room. However, it is very common that this is not the case. For most problems, you will have to do a bit more homework to gain input from others. It is almost always true that the team that is in control of the problem do not have the same understanding as customer, suppliers, or other experts.

3. MEASURE THE PROBLEM

You don't know how serious a problem is until you measure and build a baseline set of data. You will remember in a previous chapter on scorekeeping we discussed the importance of establishing a baseline so that you would then know whether or not you are improving. This will also tell you the severity of the problem.

By looking at a graph of your data you can tell many things that can guide your decisions to make improvement. For example, you may see the variations in performance, and this may point to causes of the problem. You may also see trends. In the following graph you will see three different lines. One of them demonstrates relatively stable performance. Performance is not the same every day; it varies, but it varies in a way that tells you that it is not getting better or getting worse. The other two trend lines show increasing performance or declining performance. It is extremely

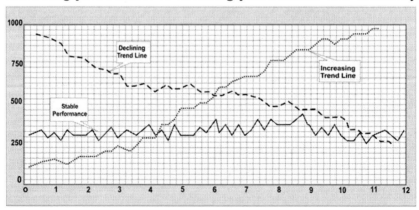

important that you observe the slope of the trend line before trying to make changes.

If your performance is in an improving trend, should you make a change at all? Perhaps it would be better to let the data continue to improve under the current conditions. Eventually it will come to a level at which it will stabilize or start to decline. If you implement an improvement, while the trend line is already improving, you will have no way to know whether or not your change has had any affect. On the other hand you may wish to make some change quickly to stop a declining trend. However, you should analyze the causes of this decline to understand what conditions are driving down performance.

4. PRINCIPLES: WHAT IS IMPORTANT?

As your team is about to solve a problem, it will be helpful if you ask the team, "What is important to make a solution successful?

For example, you may recognize that a solution will require cooperation from other teams or from managers or staff. Therefore, you may decide that a principle for an effective solution is *"We will seek buy-in by inviting those interested managers and staff to contribute to our analysis and solution."* Or, your organization may have strategic goal, for example to reduce costs, and you may decide that a principle is *"The solution must contribute to cost reduction."*

Principles are based on an understanding of the context, what is happening in your organization or sometimes the political reality of the organization. These things, in addition to the needs of your customers, define what is important.

When looking for problem-solving principles, you should go back to the team's principles and purpose you established in one of the first steps in the team process. How do those values affect the problem you are trying to solve? What other principles should guide your search for a solution?

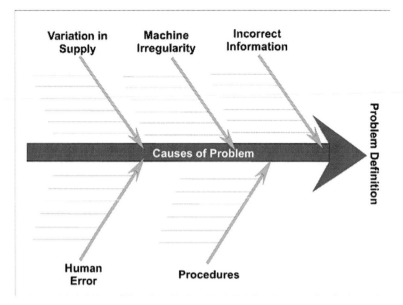

5. ANALYZE (BRAINSTORM) CAUSES OF THE PROBLEM

At this stage you will want to have your team brainstorm all of the possible causes of the problem. Probably the most effective tool for brainstorming causes and solutions is the "fishbone" or "cause-and-effect" diagram. On the following diagram you can see five major categories of potential causes. The original categories were Man, Machine, Materials and Methods. These are not necessarily the most appropriate ones for your team and for this problem. Your team should discuss and reach consensus on the four to six most likely big potential categories of causes. Then, under each of these brainstorm the possible causes.

It is usually assumed that this brainstorming will occur in one meeting. However, this may not be the best way to discover causes or solutions to problems. CEDAC is "cause-and-effect-diagrams with the addition of cards". The idea is to put a large fishbone diagram on the wall where everyone can see it. Sometimes it may be in the hall where associates arrive or leave work. On this diagram place the definition of a major problem. In an envelope by the diagram, place a set of large 3"X5" notes. Have notes of two different colors. Indicate a code that blue, for example, are the "cause" cards; while yellow may be "solution" cards. Team members can then think about the problem and place cards there whenever they like. The visibility of this diagram will encourage frequent thinking about the problem. Getting people to think is half of the solution.

Another way to brainstorm is to use an "affinity diagram." This is also a very simple idea. Again, use Post-it-Notes. Members of the team write down what they think are the likely causes of the problem. Each cause is written on a separate note. The team members then go up to a bare wall and post the notes on the wall in a random manner.

After members have been given some time, perhaps fifteen minutes, the facilitator then asks them to silently sort them into "like" causes. These like causes may be categories like those on the fishbone diagram. They are organizing the causes into "affinity" groups.

It is contrary to the group's habits to work in silence. But there is a magic to silence. People have to think! Very often we talk first and think later. Now we are being asked to think first, and we will talk later.

The members of the team will move the notes into clusters that they think go together. If one member thinks a note belongs in a different cluster, it can be moved there. If someone else moves it back, then the team may recognize that it can logically belong in more than one cluster, and a duplicate can be made.

Once the group is finished, it is time for a discussion of the different clusters.

Why are they clustered together?

What is the common idea or principle that holds a cluster together?

Are the notes truly separate causes or do some of them overlap or duplicate each other?

What are we learning from this?

Are some clusters more important than others? Or are some of them related to each other.

REACHING CONSENSUS ON PRIORITIES

Now that you have generated many possible causes of a problem, it is time to narrow them down to a critical few. You may also wish to study them further. But, first narrow them so you can focus your energy on solving the most important causes of a problem.

Here is a simple way to reach consensus on priorities.

Narrow the List: Let us assume that you have a flip chart with a list of twenty-five possible causes of the problem you are trying to solve. Ask the team members to look at this list and pick the five that they think are the most significant causes of the problem. The facilitator can ask the members of the group to come to the flip chart, take a magic marker, and make a small dot by each of the five they have selected. When they have all voted, it will be easy to see which five received the most votes.

At this point it is a good idea to ask the group "Do you all agree that these five are the five most significant priorities for us to work on? Does anyone want to make a case for something else?" Generally, the group will agree, but sometimes someone will feel strongly about another one, and it may be that others do not understand the issue in the same way that he or she does. You can ask the group if they agree to add this as a sixth item.

Now you can decide whether five are too many to pursue further. You may want to get the list down to the two causes to really focus your energies. If this is the case, you can now ask the group to vote again. But, before voting a second time, it is a good idea to ask someone to argue the case for each of the causes remaining on the list. This is often a healthy discussion in which one or two members may be able to provide information that only they have.

REACH CONSENSUS

Either by voting again, or by a simple show of hands, you may now reach consensus. When reaching consensus, it is important for the leader or facilitator to state the decision being made and ask everyone if they agree. The facilitator should simply look at the group and see if all are nodding their heads. If not, the facilitator should seek clarification.

PARETO ANALYSIS

The other, and more scientific, way to prioritize is to do a Pareto Analysis. The above process of prioritizing may be based entirely on how the members of the team "feel" about different causes of the problem. Sometimes those feelings are well grounded, and sometimes they are not.

To do a Pareto Analysis you must have data on the different causes of the problem. Once you have narrowed the potential causes down to five or ten, you may decide to go collect data to determine exactly how often the problem is caused by each.

Let's use the example of a team of employees who work in a movie theater. They have a form at the exit from the theater on which customers are encouraged to give feedback. You have taken the cards for a one month period and sorted all of the complaints. Here is the list of complaints and the number of each. You will also see the percent this represents of the total.

1. Dirty floors in theater – 97 (45.3%)
2. Dirty rest rooms – 65 (30.3%)
3. Movie started late – 27 (21.6?)
4. Bad popcorn – 13 (06%)
5. Discourteous employees – 7 (.03%)
6. Temperature in theater – 5 (.02%)

    Total = 214 complaints

214 complaints equal 100% of the total complaints. Below you can see a bar graph representing the number of complaints by category and a line representing the total percent represented by each column, cumulatively, so it ends at 100%.

Looking at this chart, you can see that the first two "critical few" causes represent 75% of the total complaints. If you could eliminate those two problems you would have eliminated 75% of the causes of dissatisfaction on the part of customers. It may be possible to focus on all of the problems. However, on many teams it is not possible to focus on everything at once; rather it is most effective to pick one or two on which to focus your energies. Pareto analysis has proven an effective way of prioritizing problem-solving efforts.

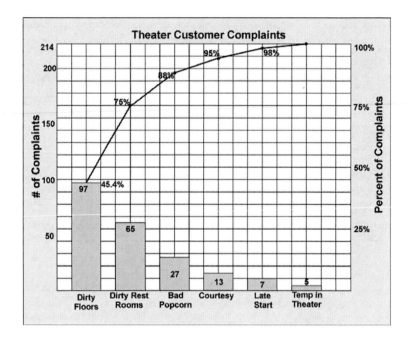

6. Brainstorm Solutions

You have now gathered a great deal of information on your problem. You have thought about it a great deal. Now it is time to think about and define solutions.

Start by brainstorming solutions. Use the same brainstorming techniques, including the fishbone diagram, affinity diagram and other techniques but this time in a search for solutions to the specific causes you have defined.

It is wise to NOT feel that you have to decide on a solution in one meeting. Often you need to study solutions. You may need to consult with an engineer if the solution involves changes in equipment. You may need to consult with human resource professionals regarding the need for additional training if that is part of your solution.

When you consider solutions, consider experimenting. Do not assume that you have to "bet" that you have made the one right decision. It is dangerous to tie your ego to a solution. Even with the best problem-solving methods, we are often wrong. It is okay to be wrong if you are willing to take action, evaluate, learn, and modify your solution. Thomas Edison tried thousands of "solutions" before inventing the light bulb. There is no reason to think that you will discover the one "right" solution on your first try. If you become too invested in one solution, it may make you blind to other opportunities or other solutions.

7. ACTION PLANNING – TAKE ACTION

Now you have to be a manager. You have to manage the implementation of solutions. This is not difficult, but it requires a disciplined approach. On the following page you will find an Action Planning Worksheet that will be helpful.

Every action plan should include the following simple elements:

What Action Needs to be Taken:

Who will take the action:

When will the action be completed?

Status: Following the development of this action plan, it should be reviewed at each meeting of the team.

8. CONTROL FOR RESULTS AND REVIEW

Control simply means to continue measuring your process and results. This is why you have a scorecard. You should now see changes on your graphs. If not, then why not?

Solving problems almost always requires repeated analysis and brainstorming solutions. You should never feel like a failure when you do not get the results you hoped for. Be a scientist. Learn from your results, experiment again, watch the results again, and you will discover the best solution.

Action Plan			
Problem:			
Solution:			
Action-What?	**Who Will Act?**	**When?**	**Status**

CHAPTER *16*

Motivation and Human Performance

Human motivation is a subject on which there have been more theories developed and more books written than almost any other. Debates about the source of motivation go back to the Greek philosophers, Plato and Aristotle. Much of the debate about motivation has been about whether motivation comes from within or is the result of outside forces in the environment. Entire schools of psychology have grown up around these two ideas.

It is safe to say that human motivation is complicated and there are a lot of individual and cultural differences in how we are motivated. But there are also some universal motivations although they may appear different in different cultures. One way to understand motivation is to consider that there are three levels of motivation: the spiritual, the social and the situational.

MOTIVATIONS OF THE HUMAN SPIRIT

The spiritual level of motivation refers to those things that are very deep personal beliefs and values. Your religious faith, your family, and your country may all be sources of motivation at this spiritual level. Motives at this level are almost always focused on the very long term. You will sacrifice for achieving a goal in the afterlife. You will sacrifice much of your own pleasure for the well-being of your family. And many have willingly sacrificed their own lives for their country and their faith.

While no one at work will ask you to sacrifice your life, there are still spiritual motivations in the world of work organization. Knowing that your company has a sense of purpose, is doing something worthy for society, and is creating a positive legacy is important. It is not something that you will see reported in this month's scorecard, but it is something that will cause people to make sacrifices for the organization. We all want to know that we work for a "good" company.

SOCIAL MOTIVATIONS

Social motivations are those that define who you are in relation to other people. It is innate in the human species to seek friendship, family, association, and a respected status among those whom we value. There are not many among us who would want to go live on a mountain top by ourselves as the proverbial "mountain

man." It may seem like an interesting escape for a short time, but most of us could not stand the loneliness and isolation for long.

Anyone who has served in a prison isolation cell or as a prisoner of war will tell you that the absence of human contact almost drove them mad. To associate with others is a fundamental human need. The quality of those associations is something we strive to improve throughout our lives.

Just as the family farm and craft shop were a strong source of social support one hundred years ago, the work or management team, as well as the larger social network in our organization, can serve as a system of needed social support. A healthy social system tends to make individuals psychologically healthy. A dysfunctional social system creates personal dysfunction. This rule can easily be seen in the social system of the family. We all know of examples of dysfunctional families producing dysfunctional individuals.

Much of our motivation has to do with social relationships. We work for promotions not only for the increase in compensation, but also for the increase in social status. We will choose to work for a company that has higher social status than one that does not. And we will work for status within our social group. We all want the approval of our team members as well as those outside of our team. This is natural and we shouldn't try to deny or dismiss this motivation. We should make use of it to recognize contributions to the team.

SITUATIONAL MOTIVATION

Situational motivations are those that occur in a more immediate time frame. These are easier to employ to manage performance because they are more easily created and controlled.

Behavioral psychology, or *behavior analysis*, is the study of how the environment affects human behavior.[11] There is a great deal of research that clearly demonstrates that you can increase (or decrease) performance by controlling those events that come before and after behavior. This is not a new revelation, nor is it complicated rocket science.

While some lean and quality consultants argue against reward systems, both Honda and Toyota have fully embraced them. In the

---

[11] The subject of motivation, positive reinforcement or incentives is a subject of much misunderstanding in the lean and quality community. As much as I revere Dr. Deming, he contributed to a good deal of confusion by promoting the idea that incentives don't work. This was a gross over generalization and was based on his personal experience as an hourly employee at the Western Electric Hawthorne plant. His experience was with hourly piece-rate incentives and it is certainly true that these create problems and are not compatible with lean or a team environment. However, Dr. Deming did not know the data – the scientific research that has been conducted for fifty years on the relationship between behavior and environmental contingencies. There are literally thousands of scientific or academic studies that verify the power of consequence to behavior and antecedent stimuli, positive and negative, and their effect on human and animal behavior. If you want to seriously study this matter I refer you to the following academic journals: the *Journal of Applied Behavior Analysis*, the *Journal of Organizational Behavior Management*; and the *Journal of the Experimental Analysis of Behavior*. The generalization that rewards "don't work" is unhelpful to a serious effort to improve human performance and factually inaccurate.

excellent book Toyota Culture the use of a "blended and balanced rewards and recognition system" is described. [12] Twenty-five percent of salaried compensation at Toyota is bonus based on performance.

It is interesting that on that same page the authors refer to the 4-to-1 principle, the importance of using four positive comments or feedback to each one negative. I have on my desk a paperweight that says "4 to 1" that goes back to my days in the 1970's working with Aubrey Daniels and Fran Tarkenton at Behavioral Systems, Inc. As one of the first companies to teach the use of behavioral psychology in business, we taught managers to carry around 4-to-1 cards and record how many of their interactions were either positive or negative with their employees. This is the original source of this "4-to-1" idea and I am sure most at Toyota don't know its origin.

Some years ago, Dr. Ogden Lindsley, one of the pioneers of learning theory and the science of human behavior, did a research project to determine the optimum ratio of positive to negative consequences in the classroom. The results may be a bit of trivia, but the significance of the results is profound common sense.. When teachers, on the average, praised children more than they criticized them, 3.57 to 1, to be exact, they achieved the highest performance from their students. One need not meditate for long to recognize the importance of this. Adults are not very different from children in their reaction to positive consequences.

When managers are asked to measure their interactions with employees, from a positive-negative perspective, they often find that the negatives far outweigh the positives. When managers are encouraged to strive for a 4-to-1 ratio of positive to negative interactions with their employees, performance accelerates. Seek 4-to-1! Seek 4-to-1 with your children, your team members, your employees; even seek 4-to-1 when talking to yourself! High performers have positive thoughts about themselves and do not indulge in negative self-talk or self-pity.

---

[12] Liker, Jeffrey K. and Hoseus, Michael, Toyota Culture: The Heart and Soul of the Toyota Way. McGraw-Hill, New York, 2008. Page 404.

THE A-B-C MODEL

One simple way of remembering this model is to think about the A-B-C Model. The "A" is for antecedents. An antecedent is something that comes before and acts as a *prompt* for behavior. Red light, green light, stop sign and a thousand other things that we see every day are antecedents for behavior. They are intended to serve as cues or prompts for a specific behavior. The "B" is for the desired behavior, such as taking your foot off the gas and putting it on the brake at a stop sign. The "C" is for consequences. When you stop for a stop light, the consequence may or may not happen, but the chance that you will have an accident or receive a traffic ticket if you don't stop is sufficient to control our behavior. It is clear that the antecedent and the consequences in this case serve as motivation for the behavior of stopping your car.

If you have children, it is easy to think of lots of examples of antecedents and consequences that affect their behavior and sometimes don't. Think about the children cleaning up their rooms. What antecedents and consequences might have an effect on this behavior?

Antecedents are conditioned, in other words we *learn* to respond to an antecedent. What does this mean? The traffic sign on the freeway says 65MPH. How fast is the traffic going? Probably 75. Why? Because you know that if you are going 68MPH there is no consequence. Actually, there is a positive consequence for going faster than 65MPH. It is pleasurable. And you enjoy passing others more than you enjoy being passed by others. In your experience, you have learned that you are not likely to get a speeding ticket unless you are going more than 75MPH. Therefore, the antecedent stimulus that says "65MPH" actually means 75MPH in terms of behavior and consequences – or, what behavioral psychologists call the *contingencies of reinforcement*. But what would happen if

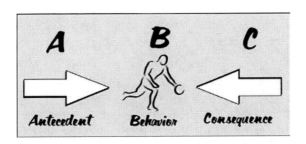

tomorrow, on the same highway, you suddenly were stopped by a policeman and given a ticket for traveling at 67MPH? You would be shocked and angry. Yes, you know the speed limit is 65, but this isn't fair! It isn't "fair" because it is a change in the consequences. If every driver, every day, were given a ticket for traveling even 66MPH, how long would it take for all the traffic to slow down to 65MPH? Only a couple days.

Now, what antecedents may work to promote studying by your child? One very powerful antecedent would be if one parent sat down with the child and read a book and suggested that they sit and read together. You do your homework, while the child does hers. Another antecedent would be saying, "OK, its homework time" and turning off the television.

But these will become effective if the child studies and then the parents provide a meaningful consequence, a positive consequence that the child will then associate with the antecedent. In other words, you sit and read with your child, and after fifteen minutes you say to the child, "I really like sitting here with you while we both read."

Imagine this situation, which is unfortunately too often typical. Mom, Dad, and their son are sitting after dinner watching *The Simpsons* on television. Ten minutes into the show Dad looks at his watch and says to his son, "Hey, Jr., isn't it time for you get upstairs and do your homework?" (Prompt #1) His son does not answer and both keep watching the TV.

Ten minutes later a commercial comes on and Dad realizes that his son is still sitting there. "Hey, I thought I said it's time to get upstairs and do your homework," he says, a bit more aggravated this time. (Prompt #2) The son says, "OK, OK, I'm going; the shows almost over."

They both go back to watching TV. Ten minutes later the show is over and they are both sitting there watching the promos for the next show. Then Dad says to his son, "Hey, UPSTAIRS, NOW!" (Prompt #3) while pointing to the stairs. The son, gets up and says, also in an aggravated voice "OK, OK, I'm going."

The way Dad is managing behavior in this situation is designed to teach his son NOT to respond to Prompts #1 and 2. He is teaching, but he doesn't realize what he is teaching. He is teaching his son that the only antecedent that he really needs to respond to is Prompt #3. Unfortunately, this teaches disrespect for authority, rather than respect. It teaches the son to wait for yelling and then respond with an angry tone of voice. This entire situation is completely unnecessary.

When you think about the antecedents in your work environment, think about the graphs, charts, and process maps that may be visible. Do these serve to prompt the desired behavior? Do you think that the size and color of these may have any effect? How could you maximize their effect?

TYPES OF CONSEQUENCES

There are three types of consequences to behavior. The first is positive reinforcement. The word "positive" doesn't refer to something you like. It refers to the *presentation*, rather than the *removal* of a reinforcing event. There is "negative" reinforcement, which does not mean punishment. It means the withdrawal of a stimulus that increases a performance. In all cases the word "reinforcement" is empirically defined by the increased frequency of a behavior. If there is no change in behavior, you cannot correctly say that you "reinforced" someone's behavior. Similarly, you cannot say that you have "taught" someone if they have not learned. You can say "I tried to teach them," but whether they were taught or reinforced is determined by whether their behavior changed.

This empirical definition, determined by an actual change in frequency of behavior, may seem like an academic difference. But it is actually very important. When you manage your process, you have learned to study and know the facts. The entire development of lean manufacturing was built on studying the facts, rather than someone's interpretations or feelings. Changing human performance is the same. You must know the facts, and act based on the facts, the data, and the frequency of behavior. In this way you become a scientist, learning what works and what does not work.

Positive reinforcement can be of many kinds. It can be social ("Thank you, I really appreciate your doing that for me!"); it can be material (a gift or money); it can be intrinsic. Intrinsic reinforcement comes from the activity itself. Eating is intrinsically reinforcing for most of us. Playing sports, doing some work rather than other kinds of work, can also be intrinsically reinforcing.

There are also neutral consequences. This is when nothing happens. But nothing happening is a consequence in itself. Imagine that you have worked very hard on a report for your manager. You were told that this was an important study, so you worked at night and on the weekend to get it done. You believe that you did a great

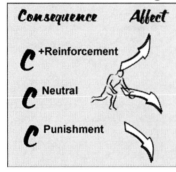

job, and you are very proud of the work you did. You then bring the report to your manager. He isn't in, but you lay it on his desk where he can't possibly miss it. A day goes by, and you hear nothing. A week goes by, and you hear nothing. A month goes by, and you hear nothing. What will be the effect on your behavior? This neutral consequence will de-

motivate you. The rate of behavior will decline. The next time you are asked to do a similar job, you will be less excited, and it is likely that you will put in less effort. Your performance has gone down. This is the effect of neutral consequences. This is also referred to in behavioral psychology as "extinction." Extinction is a good description because it is removing what gives life, what feeds, a performance. How do you extinguish a fire? You deny it oxygen. It is extinguished by the absence of the air it needs. Extinguishing behavior is the same. You deny the behavior the reinforcement that it needs to continue.

We are all familiar with punishment. Punishment is the presentation of an event that reduces the rate or frequency of a behavior. Just as reinforcement is empirically defined by a change in the frequency of behavior, punishment is also empirically defined. Punishment is only punishment if the behavior occurs less frequently. It is very, very, common for parents to behave in a way that they think is punishing when it is actually doing nothing or even reinforcing a behavior. This can happen in the workplace also.

Punishment often does not work because it does not direct the individual to some more desirable behavior that will be reinforced. It is always better to reinforce good behavior rather than punish bad behavior. Punishment has negative effects. It tends to cause the person punished to want to avoid the person and the place where they receive punishment. If they are punished in the workplace, they will want avoid the workplace. If they are punished by you, they will want to avoid you.

If you want to improve performance at work, it is essential that you create a system of positive reinforcement that will increase good behavior, behavior that contributes to the goals of the organizations.

UNDERSTANDING THE SYSTEM OF CONSEQUENCES

In all organizations, there is a system of positive reinforcement. In the society, there is a similar system. Why does government constantly change the tax code to provide a deduction for investments in oil drilling, or research, or education? Because tax deductions are a form of reinforcement, and the government uses this to strengthen effort in that direction.

Every school has a system of reinforcing good academic performance. Every sport has a scorekeeping system and a system to reinforce good performance. There is a Rookie of the Year Award, an award for the best lineman, the best quarterback, and the best special team player. There are hundreds of different types of reinforcers that are designed to reinforce many different kinds of behavior.

Why has it proven effective to have so many different types of positive reinforcement? Why not just rely on one?

The answer is that people are different. In sports you have different positions in which players are able to perform in different ways. A defensive lineman can do different things than the quarterback or a wide receiver. So to motivate all of them, there must be different kinds of measurement and different kinds of awards. Notice also in our sport that some of the awards are individual and some are team. Why is this important? If every player were only thinking about how he could win an individual award, this might work contrary to good teamwork. Similarly, in your own team environment you should have both individual and team recognition or reinforcement.

Sports are very smart about creating what in behavioral psychology are called "multiple schedules of reinforcement." In other words, at any one time, acting on your behavior, there are multiple types of reinforcement schedules. At this moment acting on your behavior there are social, material and intangible sources of reinforcement. And any of these may be either for the entire team or something that impacts an individual alone.

Write down all the different types of reinforcement that you think are operating on you as a member of your team. Remember that *intrinsic reinforcement* is something derived from the work itself. For example, learning a new skill can be reinforcing. Novelty, switching jobs, can also be reinforcing. *Social reinforcement* is any recognition that comes from other people, either from within the team or from outside the team. And *material reinforcement* is something like money, prizes, etc.

MAKING REINFORCEMENT EFFECTIVE

What are the keys to the effective use of positive reinforcement to improve individual performance?

SHAPE BEHAVIOR:

We don't learn a new language all at once. We learn it in small bites, each bite getting a bit larger and more complex than the previous one. We learn virtually everything, at least everything that is complex, by taking small steps that get larger and larger.

Reinforcing gradual improvement is called "shaping" behavior. Like a statue being made out of clay, it takes shape gradually, with repeated encouragement.

I remember when my second daughter was taking "keyboard" lessons and she called me into her room and said, "Daddy listen to this." It was Three Blind Mice, or something, but I couldn't really tell. It was an effort, but it was not exactly a concert performance. I could have said, "Well, that is not what I was hoping to get when I paid for those lessons. Call me when you can play something well!" If I had, this would have been the end of those lessons and probably any motivation for her to learn music. No! Daddy knows his job. Of course I said, "That's wonderful; it sounds like you are really learning some good songs!" and she smiled.

All parents know that you must reinforce approximations (shaping) toward a goal performance if you are going to motivate a child to learn. We are all the same. You and I need reinforcement for our efforts, for making improvement, for trying. A team will not instantly achieve its goals. But, it should be recognized for making improvement and for making the effort to improve. If it keeps trying to find improvement it will succeed.

DO IT IMMEDIATELY AND FREQUENTLY:

There is a lot of research that proves that the longer the delay, the less impact the reinforcement will have on strengthening a behavior it follows. If you reinforce immediately, the value of the reinforcement is greatest. Have you ever handed in work and waited months for feedback? When it came, you probably didn't feel any great joy.

Because immediacy matters, we need systems and habits of reinforcement that provide many opportunities for earning recognition or rewards. If there is only the monthly paycheck and an annual bonus or review, there are simply not enough opportunities to provide frequent and immediate reinforcement. Motivation depends on the immediacy and frequency of reinforcement.

PERSONALIZE IT:

What may be experienced as reinforcing by one person may not be by another. Some individuals may love to be recognized and applauded in a public gathering, while that same recognition may make others feel extremely uncomfortable. Some may consider time off from work a great reward while others would rather be rewarded with an additional assignment. Just as you think about the personal interests when buying a birthday present for someone, consider the personal interests of the individual you are encouraging in the work setting.

USE VARIETY:

We love variety in most aspects of our lives. If the same thing, words or events, are used repeatedly, they will become less meaningful. The best reinforcement is the surprise, delivered when least expected or spontaneously. Simply varying the schedule on which reinforcement is delivered can greatly increase overall performance with no additional costs.

You can vary both the type of reinforcement (what) and the schedule (when). The knowledge to vary both will significantly raise the effectiveness of your performance improvement efforts.

BE CONSISTENT:

A sense of fairness and justice results from the consistency with which reinforcement is delivered. Inconsistent use of reinforcement creates disunity. Consistency does not mean not varying reinforcement. It means providing equality of opportunity for reinforcement. Just as parents teach values by consistently approving behavior, managers teach values by the consistency in their expressions of appreciation. By rewarding improvement consistently, managers give members of the organization confidence in the values represented by that appreciation. With consistency come confidence and the elimination of fear. If employees can see that you are consistent in your approval or disapproval, they will come to trust that value.

ANALYZING HUMAN PERFORMANCE PROBLEMS

Many years ago, Robert Mager devised a model for analyzing performance problems, performance analysis, that is still extremely useful.[13] Whenever you observe a human performance problem, you can use this model to analyze the problem and define a solution.

The model essentially begins by asking the question – "Is it a **can't do** or **won't do** problem?" You will know this if you ask, "If his/her life depended on it, could he/she do it now?" If you ask me to sing opera, or play concert piano, or hit a round of golf like Tiger Woods and you told me my life depended on it, I am dead! It isn't a "want to" issue. I just cannot do those things. It does not matter how big the reward or how big the threat, I simply don't have the skills. Maybe I could have developed these skills if my parents had

---

[13] Mager, Robert F. and Pipe, Peter. *Analyzing Performance Problems or You Really Oughta Wanna*. Atlanta, CEP Press, 1997.

trained me to sing or play golf at an early age, but it is unlikely even with training. I wasn't genetically endowed with the ability to sing opera. These are "can't do" rather than "won't do" problems.

In the work setting, most "can't do" performance problems, problems of knowledge or skill, are not like singing opera. They don't require unusual genetic material, and they don't have to be developed in early childhood. They simply require training. Operating equipment, computer programming or using computer programs, making an effective sales presentation, or giving an

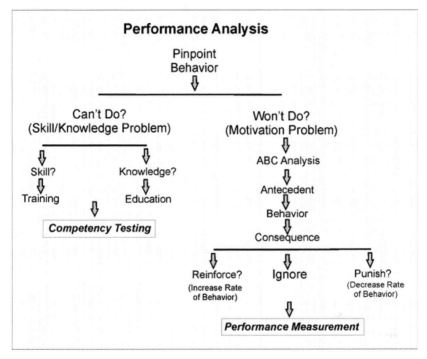

effective public talk are all skills which individuals can learn with training and practice. It is the responsibility of the manager to know which skills and knowledge are required for each job and to provide the necessary training.

It is important to recognize that one of the foundations of lean thinking and organization was developed during World War II by industry in the United States. As hundreds of thousands of men went off to war and were replaced in factories that were now asked to produce huge numbers of Jeeps, guns, ships and airplanes, it was critical to train large numbers of new workers quickly and precisely. *Training within Industry* (TWI) was developed as a precise method of teaching job skills. If your company trains workers in tasks that are repeated often, it would be useful to study and apply the TWI method.[14]

Many of the performance problems in a work setting are within the capability of employees; they just haven't been "made to matter" in a way that creates the necessary motivation. Many years ago, I was working in a textile mill in South Carolina. There was an older woman who had been there for a long time. She was known to be slow in her work but always reliable. Her rate of performance was thirty-five percent of what was called "standard-operating-efficiency." We worked with the supervisor to graph her daily performance and then suggested that he show her the graph, which was very stable, and ask her, "Mary, what do you think you could do?"

When someone is asked, in a non-threatening and positive way if they can improve, they will usually say yes. And when most people are shown data on their performance and asked, they will almost always set a higher goal. When Mary was shown her graph and she was asked what she could do, she said she thought she could do forty percent. A week later, the supervisor brought the graph back, showed it to her, and congratulated her. She was doing forty percent. Again, he asked her what she thought she could do in the next week or two. She said fifty percent. She did. Gradually, week after week, she improved her performance. To make a long story short, she got up to a steady rate of one hundred and twenty percent of standard operating efficiency. No one had ever given her specific feedback, asked her to set goals, and demonstrated sincere appreciation for her effort.

Mary's performance was not a "can't do" problem; it was a "won't do" that became a "will do" with a bit of gentle feedback and appreciation. She was capable of far more than she or anyone else would have thought. Most of us, and most teams, are capable of far more than we do.

If a problem is a "can't do" problem, it then requires the development of new skills through training, rather than motivation.

---

[14] Dinero, Donald A. *Training Within Industry: The Foundation of Lean.* New York, Productivity Press, Inc. 2005.

If the problem is "won't do," a motivation problem, then the techniques of positive appreciation or positive reinforcement can strengthen that performance.

CHAPTER *17*

LEADER STANDARD WORK

To achieve a significant change in organization culture it is necessary to reconsider the work of all employees, at all levels. One of the most common mistakes made when implementing lean culture is to assume that the change is one that must occur at the first level, and not at management levels. In fact, the changes at management levels are even more important than the changes at the first level. How managers think, act, set the example, and take personal responsibility for improvement, will determine the success of the organization.

WHAT IS LEADER STANDARD WORK?

We typically understand the need to define work expectations in very clear terms for front line employees. They are trained, evaluated, and recognized for performing their work in a standard way, a way that has proven to be effective for their job. When it comes to managers, whether first level or senior levels, we more typically assume that their work is unique, and cannot be defined in terms of any standard tasks. This is a myth. Successful CEO's of large corporations do standard things each day, week or month. They review certain sets of numbers. They contact customers. They visit operations and review performance at the operating level. They review plans and strategy. They meet with their senior management team on a regular basis to solve problems and seek improvement. There is a regular pattern to these activities that set an example and create a rhythm of forward movement in the company.

It is true that at more senior levels a greater majority of time is spent on unique activity, planning new business activity and solving larger problems. It is reasonable to assume that from the first level employee to the CEO there is a progression from more standard work to more unique work.

Leader standard work typically does the following:

- It focuses on the daily production process.
- It reviews standard work at the next level.
- It reviews operating performance and the conditions that impact operating performance.
- It considers the environment, cleanliness, and 5S.
- It includes a check on visual controls.
- It includes listening, learning, and seeking to understand.
- It incorporates the responsibility to motivate and encourage employees.
- It includes a focus on process, not just results.
- It documents the job of "lean management."

Leader standard work creates a disciplined process of management. If you are the coach of a professional football team, for example, it is important that your own behavior creates a model of disciplined action. You expect your players to eat properly, run a certain amount each day, and practice their routines and plays, in a disciplined manner. They are like the front line workers in an organization. By seeing that you adhere to a disciplined process of management yourself, this encourages them to do the same. Military officers understand this same principle. You cannot expect better behavior below than you demonstrate yourself.

Position	% Time Devoted to Standard Work
Executive Management	5-15%
Plant Management	15-25%
Area or Department Managers	20-40%
Support or Technical Contributors	30-50%
Team Leaders	60-80%
Operators – 1st level	80-100%

HOW MUCH TIME IS DEVOTED TO STANDARD WORK?

There is no one right answer to how much time should be devoted to standard work. However, it is logical to assume that at lower levels a higher percent of time is devoted to standard work and at higher levels a greater percent to unique work. This is an example of how this may vary:

DECIDING ON STANDARD WORK

You should not simply copy a list of standard work from any other company. It is important that your management think through the important tasks for each position. However, at each level the focus should be on helping, facilitating, encouraging, and supporting the work of the next level below. Ultimately it is the first level workers who do the most to serve the customers and contribute to the economic value of the organization.

In a manufacturing operation standard work may include any or all of the following categories of work for leaders. These are simply offered as an example and starting point for your own consideration.

1. Observing Work Practices
    a. Observe the standard work of the next level

     b. Provide feedback.

     c. See improvement made by those doing the work.

     d. Consider changes in standard work to reflect learning.

     e. Observe errors, mistakes, failures and determine whether there is need for education or training or motivation (can't do – won't do).

     f. Ask questions to prompt thinking about improvement.

     g. Provide positive feedback (practice 4 to 1).

     h. Makes notes on possible improvement for future action.

2. Observe Performance and Visual Display

     a. View most recent measure of performance.

     b. Observe Tact time and inventory management and control.

     c. View visual display of performance data.

     d. View display of goals and progress toward goals.

     e. Ask for understanding of trends, variability, and actions affecting performance.

     f. Provide encouragement and positive feedback.

     g. Make notes on possible improvement for future action.

3. Safety and Environmental Observation:

     a. Are safety glasses, uniforms or other gear in use as appropriate?

     b. Does behavior conform to safety standards?

     c. Is 5S being practiced and up-to-date?

     d. Are materials being handled in a safe manner?

     e. Are materials being disposed of in an environmentally acceptable manner?

     f. Make notes on possible improvement actions.

4. Meeting and Problem-solving Observation for Daily or Weekly Meetings:

a. Are the right people in attendance?

b. Is the agenda prepared and followed?

c. Is the meeting facilitated in a manner that is inclusive and encourages ownership and creativity?

d. Are action plans agreed to?

e. Are action plans reviewed?

f. Is the meeting focused on key performance measures?

g. Is data analyzed to seek understanding of causes and opportunities to improve?

h. Are problem-solving tools being used?

i. Make notes on possible improvement actions.

The following pages present a worksheet that may be used in developing and maintaining leader standard work practices. This form would be developed for each level of work, including team members and senior managers.

Leader Standard Work - Worksheet

Position:	Name:	Date:		
Tasks: Work Practices		**Time of Day**	**Daily Completion**	**Weekly Completion**
1.				
2.				
3.				
4.				
5.				
6.				
7.				
8.				

Notes on possible improvement actions:

Tasks: Observe Performance and Visual Display	Time of Day	Daily Completion	Weekly Completion
1.			
2.			
3.			
4.			
5.			
6.			
7.			
8.			
9.			

Notes on possible improvement actions:

Tasks: Observe Safety and Environmental Behavior	Time of Day	Daily Completion	Weekly Completion
1.			
2.			
3.			
4.			

5.			
6.			
7.			

Notes on possible improvement actions:

Tasks: Meeting & Problem-solving Observations	Time of Day	Daily Completion	Weekly Completion
1.			
2.			
3.			
4.			
5.			
6.			

Notes on possible improvement actions:

CHAPTER *18*

CREATING UNITY OF ENERGY
AND EFFORT

In his book *Blink*, Malcolm Gladwell used the term *thin-slicing* to describe a focused intuitive knowledge that allows an apparent snap judgment. Thin-slicing is the act of relegating the decision-making process to what Gladwell calls the *adaptive unconscious* by focusing on a small set of key variables. Gladwell gives compelling examples of art experts, such as those who are able to recognize fraudulent art, even when contradicting research shows the art to be genuine. Something about it, some small clue, alerted their intuitive judgments. While this presents an interesting insight into the decision-making process, it is my observation that a very different kind of intuition is the key to leadership in an organization.

Another kind of judgment, far more essential to creating value, which I will simply call *broad-slicing* is essential to the performance of the individual, team and company. Broad-slicing is the ability to slice across an organization and see the connections, the need for solutions, which consider knowledge of the whole, knowledge that unifies the energies and effort of the members of the organization. *Broad-slicing is the presence or promotion of principles; strategic purpose; or processes that serve to create unity of energy and effort throughout an organization or culture.*

In many ways, our culture is in a period of fragmentation, dividing into ever more narrow interest groups. In our corporations, we have increasingly narrow specialization in which experts develop their own priorities, plans and even language. There is a desperate need for leadership that can unite energy and effort into one force. Such competence is essential not only for leaders, but also for all those who seek to build economic values.

Every organization should have both external and internal strategy. The external or business strategy defines the desired market position. It defines how to position products or services to serve customers in relation to the market competition. Internal strategy defines the capability of the organization that will enable achievement of the external strategy. Defining and implementing the three broad-slices of the internal strategy will inevitably generate focused effort and a sense of unified purpose toward achieving the business strategy.

THE THREE LEVELS OF BROAD-SLICING

The three levels of broad-slicing begin with the most macro principles and proceed to what may become highly specific and defined processes. At the highest level are cultural values and beliefs that form bonds of common purpose. At the second level are business strategies that cause all work to support shared goals. At the third level are either the detailed core work processes, a chain of activities that flow from the earliest creation of input to the final satisfied customer.

Unifying values, cultural principles, language or religion all

The Three Broad-Slices of Organizational Strategy

Level 1
Unifying Values/Beliefs — Cultural Integration

Level 2
Unifying Strategies — Brand/Capability

Level 3
Unifying Processes — Operational

serve the need for cultural integration. In the political world, it is the difference between the liberation of Poland and the liberation of Yugoslavia, and possibly that of Iraq. The people of Poland were keenly aware of the broad-slices that linked them as a people – language, religion, common history and culture. In Yugoslavia, these unifying mechanisms operated in reverse and we know the result in Bosnia, Croatia and Kosovo. Today we are witnessing the struggle to create broad-slices across Iraq that may be able to hold the three primary populations together in some form of unified whole. Any country must be held together by either authoritarian force (former Iraq, Soviet Union, etc.) or by the existence or creation of broad-slices, common goals, interests, needs, philosophy or religion, that create an internal desire for affiliation. Unity of a people is ultimately a voluntary act. To be successful, the leader must elicit this voluntary response by articulating and promoting mechanisms of unity.

In companies such as Dell, Honda or General Electric there are ideas, cultural principles, which serve as unifying mechanisms in ways very similar to those in national cultures. Honda's "racing spirit" and their core competence in engine technology are broad-slices that unify the diverse business units.

Some years ago, my consultants and I worked with Chick-fil-A, in my judgment the best fast food company in the world. When you visit the Atlanta headquarters building, you may observe the cornerstone with the inscription "Dedicated to the Glory of God." The words are no mere platitude; rather their meaning permeates every function and daily life at Chick-fil-A. Their official corporate purpose is *"to glorify God by being a faithful steward of all that is entrusted to us and to have a positive influence on all who come in contact with Chick-fil-A."*

I now live in Annapolis, Maryland and when I visit the Annapolis Mall during lunchtime, there are a dozen fast food counters all handing out samples and chattering to gain your attention. Then there is the Chick-fil-A counter with four rows of three to five people deep in each row, eagerly waiting to be served. I always feel sorry for those working at the other counters.

Is there any relationship between the depth of the lines at the Annapolis Mall and the cornerstone of the headquarters building? I believe there is. Every customer knows that every Chick-fil-A store is closed on Sunday. Most know about their generous scholarship programs and other community service projects. And, of course, the food is consistently of high quality. Yet, that is not the root cause of Chick-fil-A's success. The root cause is their deeply ingrained dedication to a noble purpose – their commitment in the bonding of all employees into a set of common cultural values. This, customers can trust! Customers are attracted and loyal to a product and a brand founded on the strength of noble values.

Some years ago, Honda America Manufacturing was using one of my previous books to train their newly hired managers in the "Honda Way." When I visited Marysville, one of the striking differences in their culture was the daily team meetings held by every team and every employee, before the production line started. These meetings were to review any changes, gain the input of their associates, identify and solve immediate problems.

Sometime after one of my visits to Honda, I was speaking at one of Norman Bodek's productivity conferences. In one of the front rows, I noticed four or five men whose conference badges revealed that they were from General Motors. When I shared the example of the daily team meetings at Honda, one of them shot his arm in the air. With an air of great authority, he asked me "What is the cost benefit of those meetings if they shut the production line down for twenty minutes?"

He had me. I honestly had no idea and in front of a group of several hundreds, I told him so. He was quick to reply, "Well at GM we know the value of that line running each minute and second and you're not going to stop it unless you can demonstrate a cost benefit!"

After the conference, I returned to Marysville. Scott Whitlock was the Executive Vice President of Honda America Manufacturing and personally taught the "Honda Way" course. I told him about the above incident and I asked him if they had ever computed the cost benefit of those daily meetings. He looked at me with an expression of both disdain and distress. I was immediately embarrassed that I had asked the question. He said, "Look, we just have *faith* that if every employee and every team, every day, think and discuss how they can improve their work, it will result in better cars. I can't imagine why anyone would ask that question!"

Since this incident, more than ten years ago, General Motors market-share has shrunk and Honda's has grown. General Motors laid off workers while Honda hired. GM was insistent on cost justifying every action while Honda had faith that continuous improvement and engaging every employee in the production of high quality vehicles, would result in retaining and increasing their market-share.

The competitive advantage in both of these two cases was not some complex strategy, some technical breakthrough, or some simple technique. The competitive advantage was level one broad-slicing – the power of unifying cultural values. When you have the right values and you stick to them, like a train on tracks, it pays off in social, spiritual, and financial capital.

Broad-slices may also be a strategic direction and intention. General Electric maintains a set of values around managerial competence and accountability (a level one broad-slice) that serve to create a unifying culture. Because they have diverse business units producing aircraft engines, appliances, power generation equipment, consumer electronics and other products, it is necessary for each unit to have their own business strategy. Of course, the business strategy for selling refrigerators to Best Buys, and the strategy for selling large-scale power generating equipment to governments and major utilities, will have little in common. How then do you develop any strategic connection, and broad-slicing strategy at the second level?

General Electric has recently been promoting what they call "Ecomagination" reflecting the convergence of the need for cleaner energy, water and the development of new energy efficient technologies. This branding strategy cuts across all divisions of GE and creates a common strategic direction and purpose. Stories are a powerful tool when trying to create unified effort and the stories of innovative breakthroughs in one division can serve as a stimulus to innovation in another. Within GE, there also exists a pride, which builds loyalty in the idea that "we, GE as a company, are dedicated to the pursuit of energy efficiency."

Corporate strategy went through a period during which *portfolio management* was the preferred corporate strategy. This was the logical (or illogical) basis for conglomerates such as Textron and ITT under Harold Geneen. Geneen believed that there was no need for any link between business units owned by a corporation other than that of financial competition for the allocation of capital.

These corporations were, essentially, diversified mutual funds. This approach depleted shareholder value. The absence of broad-slices resulted in division and disintegration of these companies.

The added value of a conglomerate today, a multi-business unit corporation, resides precisely in the sharing of core competencies or capabilities – some core technology or market strategy that can add value across the business units. "Ecomagination" is a good example of this. If there is no Level Two broad-slice to create value across business units, then there is little reason for those units to exist within one company.

The merger of Time-Warner and AOL was built on the premise of creating some synergy across the combined business units. However, this was only a vague intention with no serious strategy and no appreciation for the cultural differences that inhibited the creation of genuine broad-slices. The idea of an integrating strategy is not enough. The integrating strategy must be executed effectively. If Level One cultural integration is lacking, in fact working against integration, the strategy is swimming against the current and is likely to fail. It has failed at Time-Warner. Shareholders paid the price for this lack of integrating strategy.

Shared strategy may include marketing, manufacturing or technology. The same is true for broad-slicing at Level Three – the level of process.

The focus lean manufacturing is on the horizontal flow from the first step in production to the final purchase by the end-use customer. It is one seamless, interruption free process from beginning to end and one that tears down any barrier created by legal walls (companies), departments (different functions) or by personalities, which slows down the flow, add time and costs and reduce the ability to improve quality.

In order for this *just-in-time* system to work successfully, there must be immediate communication between those assembling a product and their suppliers. Any defect in parts or components found during assembly, must be reported to the supplier immediately, usually in less than an hour. There is no time for management to review defects and meditate on their actions. The action is reflexive and requires no deliberation, no management meetings or reports.

It is easy to see how lean production unifies those in a manufacturing process. The same is true in marketing and sales, office work, and any business process.

While complex organizations require differentiation in function, they equally require unifying horizontal processes. The competence to create effective horizontal workflow is one of the most essential competitive advantages in all modern organizations. This is Level Three *broad-slicing*.

Broad-slicing is the glue that holds companies and societies together in a unified whole. The failure to recognize or create broad-slices is one reason both companies and societies fall apart. Similarly, teams and individuals fall-apart in the absence of unifying ideas that focus their energy and effort.

We have the habit of magnifying differences and ignoring that which is common. Every public discussion seems to focus on how one group is different, better, more correct, than another. When the findings of the human genome project was announced, it was revealed that the genetic composition of individuals sampled from different races was approximately 99.99 percent the same across races. Yet, it is our learned habit to focus a great deal of attention on the differences while ignoring that, which is common. Almost every tragedy of human history is a result of an obsessive focus on differences whether political, racial, religious or cultural. Like a spreading virus, this infects our work life.

Perhaps, as we first emerged from the cave, we learned that we were more likely to be attacked by those who were different, than by those who were the same as us. And we have focused on differences ever since.

At every level of our society, we are torn between the habits of division and the bonds of unity. The downfall of every civilization and corporation is not the attack of the external barbarian, but the internal disintegration and subsequent loss of will. Internal competitors, blind to their own deeds, raise the dagger and strike their own heart, thinking they are attacking their opponent but failing to realize that they are in the boat together, rapidly circling in a descending whirlpool of debate.

It is my heartfelt belief that the greatest difficulty facing our corporations, families and society are the patterns of division and disintegration. To the degree of internal conflict, the distraction blinds one to the external threats and nullifies the potential to respond. In my opinion, the number one leadership skill required in our organizations, is the ability to promote unity of purpose and energy.

The coach of every athletic team understands the essential advantage of united effort, the multiplication of energy as one member supports and encourages the other. *"Build for your team a feeling of oneness, of dependence on one another and of strength to be derived by unity.*" Vince Lombardi urged, who knew something about winning. Babe Ruth said "*.The way a team plays as a whole determines its success. You may have the greatest bunch of individual stars in the world, but if they don't play together, the club won't be worth a dime..*". Anyone who has followed sports knows the truth of these statements as very often the teams with the largest salaries and most revered players are defeated by another with great "chemistry," the magic of a unified team. And almost all work done in business and other organizations today, is ultimately the product of unified effort.

CHAPTER *19*

LEADERSHIP, LIFE CYCLES AND CULTURE

DOES YOUR LEADERSHIP STYLE MATCH THE NEEDS OF YOUR ORGANIZATION'S CULTURE?

(Note: This chapter is not essential to implementing lean culture. It is, however, a perspective on leadership and organization culture that has proven very helpful to leadership groups assessing and developing culture strategy. It provides a method of assessing personal leadership behavior and the effect on the culture. It is also a fun way to look at leadership.[15])

The history of countries, civilizations and corporations is the history of the pursuit and destruction of wealth. If wealth were "naturally" sustainable, there would have been no decline of Rome or Greece, or the Aztecs or Mayans, all once great civilization with all the wealth of their time. But they were not sustainable. They all ended in chaos and defeat. If the wealth of corporations did not contain the virus that would cause their death, there would have

---

[15] This chapter is adapted from *Barbarians to Bureaucrats: Corporate Life Cycle Strategies* and *Sustainable Wealth*, both by Lawrence M. Miller.

been no death of Enron, Lehman, Bear Sterns, and hundreds of others we forget. But the virus is there, and leaders are blind to their own disease, blinded by the illusion of financial might. It is a fragile illusion.

Mark Twain said "History doesn't repeat itself – but it does rhyme." That is probably an accurate assessment of the value of history. There are broad patterns that seem to follow some natural evolution as there are natural patterns in the birth and growth of infants, animals and even plants. There can be no exact roadmap drawn from history, but there can be wisdom derived from the patterns. The culture at the birth of a company or civilization is of one kind, and that is entirely different than the culture at maturity or in decline. The behavior of leaders, their relationships, skills and intentions are different at each age. And wealth varies by stage. Obviously, at birth a company is not rich in financial assets. But it may be rich in innovation or in the spiritual quality of dedication to a worthy purpose. In maturity a company becomes increasingly focused on the refinement of process and builds its social capital both in brand equity and internal relations. Material resources are growing, and with that growth the motivations are likely to shift from the single cause the excited the early followers to a more narrow self -interest. And as financial assets increase and managers are increasingly drawn from those who know more about finance and mechanisms of financial control, the innovative spirit declines, and social relations fragment. Companies toward their end, like civilizations, decline in a process of social disintegration, the loss of trust and innovation. The loss of money is only the last sign of decay.

Oswald Spengler in *The Decline of the West* recognized the cycle of spiritual awakening at birth and the hardening of the arteries, what we call "bureaucracy" in the emergence and decline of cultures. You can exchange the word "culture" or "civilization" with the word "corporation" in almost every instance and see the parallel.

"A culture is born in the moment when a great soul awakens out of the proto-spirituality of ever-childish humanity... But its living existence, that sequence of great epochs which define and display the stages of fulfillment, in an inner passionate struggle to maintain the Idea against the powers of Chaos without and the unconscious muttering deep-down within... The aim once attained

– the idea, the entire content of inner possibilities, fulfilled and made externally actual – the Culture suddenly hardens, it mortifies, its blood congeals, its force breaks down, and it becomes civilization."[16]

Arnold Toynbee long ago recognized that "We have ascertained that civilizations come to birth in environments that are unusually difficult and not unusually easy. The greater is the challenge, the greater the stimulus to growth." He described the role of leaders in the emergence of civilization as those who recognize the challenges presented by their environment and then muster the creative response to that very challenge. This creative response to challenge is the mechanism of growth, both in civilization and corporations. A "condition of ease" leads, not to growth, but rather to decline. Every innovation is a response to some challenge, either externally or within. The successful response leads to the new challenges of growth, size, specialization, and then organization. With growth, size, complexity and wealth come leisure time, the pursuit of leisure rather than challenge, increasing materialism, and hubris of leaders. Lacking the recognition of challenge, leaders lose their creativity and increasingly rely on yesterday's successful response in the presence of new challenges. It is this condition of ease and failure

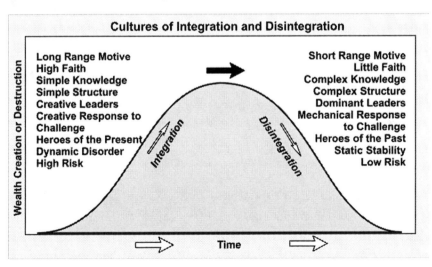

16 Spengler, Oswald. *The Decline of the West*, Volume 1 (New York, Alfred A. Knopf, 1926), p. 106.

of creativity that is the cause of decline. Too often, organizations follow a similar path.

In the life cycle of civilizations and companies there is a twin-fold process of integration and disintegration. Civilizations or companies, when growing, expand their borders and are integrating different people, ideas, competencies, and cultures. When they cease the process of integration and expansion, they start defending their borders and building walls to keep out the energetic barbarians, and the process of internal disintegration begins. As the focus shifts from offense to defense, the focus of energy is increasingly internal rather than external. The spirit of unity of purpose increasingly becomes the spirit of self-interest and internal division. Soon the body of the culture is engaged in internal warfare and self-mutilation, and the enemy does not so much conquer as to march in to fill the void created by the impotence of the old culture. Toynbee concluded that the decline of every civilization was not at the hands of an external enemy but rather an act of suicide, the loss of will, and the disintegration of the culture. Whether or not you accept Toynbee's analysis of the rise and fall of civilizations, there are clearly lessons for leaders of companies and countries. You can see these in the emerging periods of the Prophet, Barbarian and Builder and Explorer. You can also see the decay and decline beginning the dominance of the Administrator, the Barbarian and the Aristocrat. You can only hope to see an age of the Synergist, when the best qualities are held in balance.

THE PROPHETIC AGE: INSPIRATION AND INNOVATION

> *"Reasonable men adapt themselves to their environment; unreasonable men try to adapt their environment to themselves. Thus all progress is the result of the efforts of unreasonable men."* George Bernard Shaw

In the beginning is the word, the creative act, the spirit of renewal. Creative personalities, including religious prophets, seem to follow a pattern of withdrawal-and-return. They disappear into the mountains or desert. They remove themselves from the distractions of the current order and seek some vision of a better future. Their power to inspire others is only seen on their return when they are intentionally disruptive. A revolution begins and their followers can hardly be called an organization, more a group of disciples. It is disruption, not order. It is the nature of creative personalities. The vision of these prophets is like a rocket blast, a surge of energy that disturbs the old and propels movement toward something new. Often these prophets are incapable of doing their work within the framework of the old order, but must but be exiled to a new land. As new wine must be put in new bottles, so too, may the new wine of innovation require the new bottle of new organization, *(Mar 2:22 And no man putteth new wine into old bottles: else the new wine doth burst the bottles, and the wine is spilled, and the bottles will be marred: but new wine must be put into new bottles.)*

Most companies appear to be formed by the impetus of a creative personality, the *prophet,* who issues forth the creative response to challenge. The creative personality is almost never a great manager or administrator. The founders of Apple Computer or General Electric were visionaries who were devoted to their technologies, to their research, and to the creation of new products. In the "latter days" the prophets will be crucified or exiled by the bureaucrats and aristocrats who will seek to maintain order. The prophets are inherently disorderly. Disturbing the established

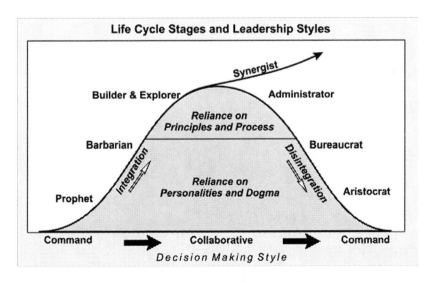

order is the business of prophets.

One must wonder whether or not Thomas Edison could find a home in the corporations that grew from his creativity. Could he survive the current General Electric Corporation?

They used to say that you could find Edison in his laboratory by following the trail of tobacco juice that he squirted onto the floor. When his wife asked him why he refused to use a spittoon, he answered that a spittoon was hard to hit, but the floor was difficult to miss. Not only did he have bad habits, but he was an all-around bad manager and poor communicator. The modern GE would likely have little to do with Thomas Edison.

When it comes to inventors, Edison is not unique. He lived in the world of ideas, ideas that he brought to tangible fruition and practical application, but only with the help of more practical personalities. "My business is thinking," Edison proclaimed. "The man who doesn't make up his mind to cultivate the habit of thinking misses the greatest pleasures in life."

What are the assets and liabilities of an organization in its earliest stage? Of course, it will vary depending upon how the organization was created and by whom. However, it is most likely that the organization will be high in the spiritual capital of a dedication to a worthy purpose and common values. It will likely have high internal sociability but little or no brand equity. It may have high innovation capital in the area of either technology or process. It is most likely that the young company is lacking in human and financial resources.

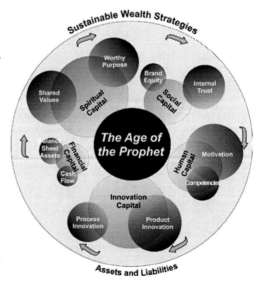

These assets and liabilities define the strengths and weaknesses of the new company. The smaller circles are those that present risks to the organization and must be developed. But they must not become the focus of the leader's energy to the detriment of the strengths. It often happens that the Prophet is the technology leader. He knows nothing about brand equity or financial management. If he devotes himself to these areas, he may weaken the very reason the organization was born. For this reason the key challenge of the Prophet is to develop internal partnerships, reliance on those who balance his or her qualities.

This diagram presents relative strengths and weaknesses, not absolute strengths and weaknesses. In other words, it may be that a large company has terrific research and development and is innovating in both technology and process. But because it has also developed strong brand equity, financial and human resources, that innovation capital will appear to be more in balance with the other forms of capital. An organization is at risk when it is out of balance. The age of the Prophet is a high risk stage precisely because the new organization has not developed a balanced wealth profile. It may have terrific technology innovation with financial value, but it may be out of business and bankrupt the next day due to the absence of cash flow. Or it may have no human competence in the area of marketing and therefore fail to develop brand equity. It is not unusual for motivation to exceed competence in the early stages and the reverse may be true in the later stages of the life of a company.

Wealth strategy is founded on the recognition of current assets and liabilities. It creates a practical plan to build balance in the organization. If an organization's wealth profile looked like the one above, it would be logical to focus strategic planning on each of the smaller circles while at the same time assuring that the leaders nurture and maintain their asset base.

The wealth profile, as can be seen in this illustration, is severely out of balance at this early stage. The degree of imbalance equals the degree of risk to the organization. The struggle for a "good life" is the struggle to achieve balance. An individual who focuses all his energy on social relationships at the expense of developing competencies will suffer. He who focuses all energies on material pursuits in disregard to spiritual values and a worthy purpose will soon find himself in an unhappy state. Organizations and civilizations have proven to be no different. Every civilization has begun its rapid descent into chaos when it was at the peak of its material achievement. The leading indicators of innovation, spiritual and social capital had already declined and were being neglected. The work of the organization is to bring itself into balance to achieve sustainability.

In the age of the Prophet the wealth that is created, and upon which the organization depends, is innovation capital in the form of a new technology or innovative process that serves customers in a superior manner. Organizations are most likely born with the dedication to some larger purpose, and the Prophet leader is likely to articulate a strong set of values that will be adopted by the members of the organization. The deficits are most likely few financial resources or human resources. While there may be strong internal sociability, trust and teamwork, there is likely little social capital in the market place. That will come later.

As we know, a majority of organizations die a natural and early death. Like the seed blown by the wind, their potential is never realized because they have not found the balance of resources (financial and human) that will nourish their development.

You may be a Prophet if...
- Your ideas are long range and visionary.
- You are willing to make great sacrifices in time and energy to see your ideas realized.
- You tend to withdraw for long periods to work through your ideas.
- You see challenges others don't see.
- Others see you as a bit "different," (You were not most popular in high school!)
- You're probably not very well organized, and you are impatient with details and administration.

Your organization may be in the Prophet stage if...
- Your leader is a visionary and creative person on whose ideas the company was founded.
- Your organization is at risk because it has not yet proved its product's viability in the marketplace.

- There is more chaos than organization, with things changing daily, reporting relationships unclear, and processes undefined.
- There is an excitement and deep belief in what you are trying to accomplish.

THE BARBARIAN AGE: CRISIS AND CONQUEST

*"To be a successful soldier, you must know history...
What you must know is how man reacts. Weapons change,
but man, who uses them, changes not at all. To win battles,
you do not beat weapons – you beat the soul of the enemy
man."* George S. Patton IV

The prophet founders of companies are soon followed by, or become themselves, *barbarians*, the commanding generals whose strength of will focuses energy in crisis. The idea and inspiration is not enough. Decisive action is now required to build a company. Every new company is in a crisis, a fight for survival. When business is in a fight for survival it has more in common with war than many managers realize. The ability to move quickly, with discipline and unity of energy and effort, is the key to victory.

The early time of a company's growth is inevitably a time of crisis, and what is needed most are leaders capable of acting in crisis, more so than those able to gain broad consensus. While barbarians lead the conquering march, their talents will soon be out of date. They are good when their focus does not require the coordination of complexities or working through the subtleties of political decision-making or power. It is why General Patton was great in combat and a huge bother off the field of combat. Ray Kroc, the founder of McDonald's, did not create the innovation upon which the company was built. But he did take that innovation and lead it on a conquering march. He was entirely focused on "quick, clean and courteous", the three simple qualities on which the company was built. He would visit stores and immediately visit the bathroom. As chairman of a company with thousands of restaurants, he would immediately barge through the door to the cleaning supplies and would scrub down the toilets and mop the floor. Insane? Perhaps -- but he did it. He built the company with this fierce focus that a General Grant would well understand. The barbarians are always very close to the real work of the organization and are able to understand in simple terms what matters most. This will later be lost.

The Barbarian will make two appearances in the life cycle of a company – immediately after the birth of the business and again during times of renewal, when the excess of the baggage of bureaucracy must be shaken loose and swept away. His forte is discipline and rapid action.

While the Prophet is the first leader/visionary, the Barbarian is the first leader/manager. He brings others into the organization; he assigns roles and responsibilities; he directs action toward goals; he rewards and corrects. His manner is not one we associate with contemporary management. This Barbarian is a command decision maker, unlikely to consult others or form consensus. This is Genghis Khan, Attila the Hun, and Alexander the Great. They literally rode at the front of their cavalry in battle and suffered wounds with their men. They had an intimate relationship with the first level of their army, those who determined the fate of the battle. Alexander loved his army and, as is always the case, loved returned in an organization is called loyalty. Alexander's army was as devoted to him as he was to them. This is the magic chemistry of the heroic leader, and when the office towers are built and the leaders retreat to the top floor to remove themselves from the mess of the battle, they will not understand what happened to loyalty. They will fail to recognize that it is they, themselves, who lost the love for those who do the work and the reaction of those on the front line is only response to their stimulus.

Heroic leadership, because it has so much to do with emotion rather than analytic decision-making, has much to do with symbols. The heroic leader understands, whether through intelligence or intuition that the external impression presented to his followers is as important as any decision he makes. He knows both his followers and adversaries will study his every move, and those moves will be theatrically orchestrated for their effect. And if he has any doubts about the battle plan, they will never show. Historian John Keegan said it well:

"Heroic leadership is like priesthood, statesmanship, even genius, a matter of externals almost as much as internalities. The leader of men in warfare can show himself to his followers only through a mask, a mask that he must make for himself, but a mask made in such a form as will mark him to men of his time and place as the leader they want and need."[17]

The Barbarian is the leader in the age of warfare, whether on the field of battle or business. Corporations may find themselves in a desperate fight for survival during their early years and again after they have been lulled to sleep by their size and success and set upon by a more aggressive challenger. The best turnaround artist, the executive most able to reinvigorate a deteriorating culture is the Barbarian.

When Steven Jobs returned to Apple Computer after his period of exile from the company, he returned to reinvigorate more than the technology. He had to reinvigorate the human spirit, the faith in the original spirit and purpose of Apple. He was not the model of consensus decision-making because he knew where he wanted to take the company, what was important, and what was not important. When Lee Iacocca took charge of Chrysler he was the same.

Barbarians are well suited to the requirements of battle and ill-suited to the complexity of mature organizations in which consensus reaching across organizational lines is essential. Our culture places high value on communications and empathy. Certainly these are important but not in times of war. It is also a period when disorder, a necessary level of chaos, is essential and the approach of the Administrator who values order and stability will result in failure. When we went to war in Vietnam, we followed a Secretary of Defense, Robert McNamara, who had a Ph.D. in Administration from Harvard and had led Ford Motor Company from a period of chaos to a period of control by accountants and strategic planners. If filing cabinets and planning could have won the war, we would have been victorious. Unfortunately, we were fighting someone who said "You will kill ten of my men for every one of yours we kill; but it is you who will tire of it first." Ho Chi Minh was a Barbarian, and when a Barbarian meets Bureaucrat on the battle field the war is over before the fighting has begun. Ho Chi Minh understood what General Patton understood when he said, *"Weapons change, but man changes not at all; you beat the soul of the enemy man."*

---

[17] John Keegan, *The Mask of Command* (New York: Viking, 1987), p.11.

The organization of this heroic age is more like the military organization than the lean manufacturing organization lauded today. Little attention has been paid to making processes interruption free and controlled by front line teams. That will come with time. The absence of organizational process and principles is due to the reliance on personality. In its early days a company or civilization tends to be driven by strong personalities. In the middle, more mature and stable periods, there is greater reliance on principles and process, a Constitution and the rule of law, rather than the will of personality.

What is the wealth created during the age of the Barbarian? The wealth profile, as was true in the previous stage is not in balance during the Barbarian stage. However, it has begun to change. This is the great age of rapid expansion. Market share is being captured. This means that brand value is being created, external social capital is the most important territory conquered. But, at the same time the company must be building its human resources. The number of people is growing and the organization is increasingly hiring people with specialized competence. This will be the primary focus in the next stage. Hopefully, the Barbarian is maintaining the unifying effect of Spiritual Capital, a focus on worthy purpose and shared values. And, the financial capital of the firm must be growing during this stage.

You may be a Barbarian if...
- Your mission is clear and urgent. Conquer or die is the priority.
- You are in charge and very comfortable making decisions.
- Others accuse you of being authoritarian and not consulting them on decisions.
- You are very action-oriented and have little patience with planning and administration.

Your organization may be in the Barbarian age if...
- It is rapidly expanding, taking in new territory and integrating the conquered.

- Decisions are made quickly and the leader may only consult a small group of associates.
- Growth in products and markets is far ahead of the growth in administration, processes and organization structure.
- The demand for performance is high and those who can't are left behind or expelled.

THE AGE OF THE BUILDER AND EXPLORER: SPECIALIZATION AND EXPANSION

> *"Insofar as civilization grows and continues to grow, it has to reckon less and less with challenges delivered by alien adversaries and demanding responses on an outer battle field, and more and more with challenges that are presented by itself to itself in an inner arena. In other words, the criterion of growth is progress towards self-determination."*
> Arnold Toynbee

The period of the Prophet may be a brief moment in the history of the corporation. The age of the Barbarian should also be short. If an organization's leadership remains in the Barbarian Age, its growth will be arrested. It must move on and enter a period of specialization, a time when systems and structure take form, and the organization matures.

Now leadership has to take on a different character. It must be shared, delegated, and increasingly collaborative. While the leaders must continue to be creative and fast moving, they must also develop increasingly specialized competence in production, service, marketing, and sales. If they do, this third stage may last for centuries in the life of civilization and decades for a corporation.

The primary leaders in this period of specialization are the Builder and Explorer. The Builders will construct the internal capacity of efficient production, while the Explorers continue the push outward, expanding the boundaries of the developing corporation or culture. In civilization the Builders are literally building cities, roads, reservoirs, libraries and stadiums; the Explorers are conquering new territory to expand the scope and influence of the culture by integrating diverse people. In corporations the Builders are creating the means of production, they are making production efficient. The Explorers are out conquering new customers and territories, seeking to dominate their competition.

In the first two stages of development, growth is highly dependent upon the individual leader, the Prophet and the Barbarian. But in the third stage, the environment – both internal and external – is becoming too complex for such centralized decision-making.

Initially there was room for only one Christ, Mohammed or Buddha on stage at any one time. But as society becomes more integrated, including increasingly diverse people, it is necessary that some degree of pluralism, the mechanisms of unity and diversity, are accepted to maintain the union of diverse peoples. Now less charismatic characters must share the stage and if one personality insists on domination, he cripples the culture with internal warfare. At this stage a company has marketing, sales, engineering and manufacturing relying on the administrative functions of accounting, human resources, and information systems management. These functions must work together. Their varied interests must be taken into account. It is for this reason that some form of democracy or some form of collaborative decision-making is always formed as civilization moves up the curve towards its period of maturity and balance. The failure to make this transition in decision-making style is a primary reason for failure at this stage.

The personality required of leaders in this stage can well be seen in the great Explorer, Ferdinand Magellan. If you ever doubt that man can act with courage of heroic proportions, you need look no further than the sixteenth century explorers. Here were men who possessed not only great vision and courage, but great confidence in their ability to manage complex human affairs. The story of Magellan illustrates the combination of personal courage and competence, as well as the ability to communicate and cooperate, that are demanded in this age.

Magellan was a Portuguese who, as a young man, had served in his country's navy. At the time, ships en route to the Spice Islands sailed around Africa, but Magellan believed that a strait existed would allow westward passage, and he wanted to find it. Portugal's king, Manuel, refused to fund a search, so on October 20, 1517,

Magellan arrived in Seville to offer his services to Charles V, Grandson of Ferdinand and Isabella, and the newly crowned King of Castile.

Charles, who had adopted the motto "Plus ultra" meaning "more beyond," ultimately accepted the offer. What kind of man had he decided to fund? Historian Edward G. Bourne summarized Magellan and his feat this way:

"There was none of the prophetic mysticism of Columbus in the make-up of the great Portuguese. Magellan was distinctly a man of action, instant, resolute, enduring... the first navigation of the Straits of Magellan was a far more difficult problem of seamanship than crossing the Atlantic... Columbus's voyage was over in thirty-five days; but Magellan had been gone a year and weathered a subarctic winter before the real task began – the voyage over a trackless waste of waters exactly three times as long as the first crossing of the Atlantic... Magellan is to be ranked as the first navigator of ancient or modern times, and his voyage the greatest single human achievement on the sea."[18]

The Builder and Explorer stage of development is unlike the previous ones. Now the leader must gain the support and approval of others. Even then, there was a committee. It was the Casa de Contratacion, the official board that handled most of Spain's colonial affairs, similar to the corporate committees for capital authorization to which division managers must present expansion plans today. The Casa de Contratacion heard Magellan's plan but was unimpressed and denied approval.

Magellan then began lobbying to reverse the committee's decision. He sought the approval of Juan Foncesca, bishop of Burgos and the committee's most influential member. Foncesca's approval was obtained on the condition that his own relatives and favorites be made captains on Magellan's ships. There were three attempted mutinies during the trip, and historians suspect that those who tried to take over the expedition were acting with the bishop's encouragement.

Another member of the committee, Juan de Aranda, demanded a 20 percent cut of the expected profits in exchange for helping

---

[18] Edward G. Bourne, quoted in Morison, *The Great Explorers* (New York: Oxford University Press, 1978), p. 427.

reverse the committee's vote. No Prophet or Barbarian could survive all the manipulation, coordination, and cooperation required of Magellan and the other great Explorers in accomplishing their mission.

But accomplish it Magellan did. He sailed south and eventually found the strait that now bears his name. He circumnavigated the globe, uncertain where or when he might find a passage to the Pacific, totally ignorant of the immense size of that ocean, which is twice as large as the Atlantic and without any of the navigational equipment we now take for granted. Magellan succeeded, not because he was simply courageous, but because he attended to all of the details of keeping hour-by-hour logs, taking constant sightings of celestial bodies, and mapping every landfall and detail of the oceans he explored. He had the mind of an engineer or scientist as well as commanding skills of the general.

At the same time in history that Magellan was exploring the seas; Builders were creating the process of manufacturing and studying efficiency. The same division and the same combination of skills are required at this stage of development in the corporation.

The wealth profile of the organization in this stage is moving toward balance. Now is the time of greatly expanded human resources competencies. Innovation must shift to processing innovation and how efficiency is gained in manufacturing and sales, as well as maintaining the progress of technical innovation. The task of maintaining Spiritual Capital requires far greater skills than in the earlier days. Maintaining unity of purpose and common values is not so easy in a diverse organization with geographically dispersed units of production and sales. In the early days, common purpose was a natural result of marching into battle together. Now it must be promoted with deliberation. Also in this age, external social capital, brand equity, is greatly expanded as the marketplace both expands and recognizes the value of the organization's innovation and manufacturing competence. Of course, financial capital is now emerging as a major asset, one that can be employed for further expansion and innovation.

If the Builder and Explorer are successful, a period of balance of wealth will be achieved. But this balance is rarely maintained as there are natural forces that will push it toward bureaucracy.

You may be a builder if...

- You enjoy the "real work" of your company, making the product or delivering the service.
- You enjoy measuring the results of your work.
- You like to make decisions quickly, take action, and see results.
- You know you are not a visionary and don't waste a lot of time dreaming about the future.
- You don't like committees or sitting around wasting time talking.

You may be an Explorer if...

- You are a convincing and enthusiastic communicator.
- You sometimes feel that you work for you customers and others in your own company often seem to be obstacles to your goal of serving your customers.
- You believe your company should place a high priority on expansion.
- You are curious and you naturally explore for new opportunities for your company.
- You love to keep score, and you are competitive by nature.

Your organization is in the Building and Exploring Age if...

- Your products or services have proven to have a competitive advantage and you are growing rapidly.
- You are now profitable and you can add needed staff to develop management systems and to make processes routine and stable.
- You are hiring more, and the jobs are becoming more specialized.
- There is a high confidence in the future.

THE AGE OF THE ADMINISTRATOR: CREATING SYSTEMS, STRUCTURE AND SECURITY

"Whenever an individual or a business decides that success has been attained, progress stops." Thomas Watson, Sr. (Founder, IBM)

"The arrested civilizations have achieved so close an adaptation to their environment that they have taken its shape and colour and rhythm instead of impressing the environment with a stamp which is their own. The equilibrium of forces in their life is so exact that all their energies are absorbed in the effort of maintaining the position which they have attained already, and there is no margin of energy left over for reconnoitering the course of the road ahead, or the face of the cliff above them, with a view to a further advance." Arnold Toynbee

Increasingly the challenge is within, not from the external environment. Increasingly the leaders are seeking to bring order to the chaos of differentiated organization created in the previous stage. Counting and recording, systems and structure, are now important. And increasingly the processes of administration become dominant in their minds, and the leaders are drawn from the administrators. In time, with Administrators in charge, counting and recording become more important than the substance and spirit of creativity, the response to the external challenge that was the source of initial growth. Increasingly the focus is on internal, rather than external, challenges. The unchecked priorities of administration will soon lead to bureaucracy.

It is difficult to accept that chaos is good. But growth, in people or cultures, implies some degree of chaos. If you want a perfectly clean and orderly house, do not have children. Children, in their most rapid periods of growth, are a mess, and create a mess around them. Mess is good. In old age, the personality becomes obsessed with order and control. Just as the bones become brittle, so too does the mind become intolerant of innovation. But, there is a middle ground, a balance between the disorder of growth and innovation and needs of administering differentiated organization.

Initially administration serves the needs of those producing and selling, building and exploring. To manage a large manufacturing or selling organization you must know where things are, how many you have, and what they cost. Initially, to "take account" is to assist those engaged in the work that serves customers. But it shifts, and it gradually appears that those producing and selling increasingly come to serve those administering. It is the turning of this tide that signals the entry into the Administrative stage.

In this fourth stage, the corporation is holding its ground, creating and maintain order. And now the successful leaders face their single greatest test. Are they able to maintain forward motion, continue to be creative, decisive, and develop increasing competence, while at the same time administering secured territory? If they can, the organization will break through to that ideal balance that assures continued health. If they can't and the Administrator becomes the dominant leader, imposing his cultural priorities, decline will begin.

To survive this stage, managers must understand and employ both leadership and management. Leadership provides the vision, values, and purpose that create motion. Management channels the energy leadership creates. Leadership is necessarily a personal relationship; while management is necessarily less personal and more systematic. One appeals to the intuition and emotion, the other to rational intellect. Both are needed, and they are needed in balance.

Can there be heroes of administration? It seems almost an oxymoron. However, the history of commerce demonstrates that administrators have overcome great challenge to enable organizations, even nations, to achieve great things.

The American West was not conquered by the pioneers and the cavalry alone. The development of the great railroads that moved from east to west was essential to the integration of the westward territories into the United States. The railroads were the prototype of the large American corporation. They were the first to require coordination of resources and schedules across a large territory and thus demanded great numbers of full-time managers. It was these railroad managers who first developed what we regard as modern administrative practices to coordinate, control, and evaluate the activities of scattered operating units. The resulting efficiencies, later adopted by the nation's production and service organizations, are largely responsible for the global expansion of corporations over the past century.

Following their rapid growth, and due to the capital intensive nature of railroads, the railroad companies began to merge. In the early days of railroads, each local railroad company decided which gauge of track to lay. Moving goods a great distance required unloading the goods from cars of one railroad and re-loading them onto cars of the next railroad that would carry them the next distance. Integration and efficiency require some degree of uniformity. From a "do your own thing" entrepreneurial culture that initially created rail lines, now control and conformity were essential to gain economic efficiency.

The various lines along the Erie Canal and the Hudson River were consolidated in 1853 to form the New York Central Railroad. Daniel C. McCallum of the Erie railroad was promoted to general superintendent of the new line and charged with creating a smoother running organization. He developed a system of prompt reporting of both personnel activity and the movement of rail cars that had no precedent.

In 1854 the American Railroad Journal reported: "By an arrangement now perfected, the superintendent can tell at any hour in the day, the precise location of every car and engine on the line of the road and the duty it is performing. Formerly, the utmost confusion prevailed in this department, so much so, that in the greatest press of business, cars in perfect order have stood for months upon switches without being put to the least service, and without its being known where they were. All these reforms are being steadily carried out as fast as the ground gained can be held."

Daniel C. McCallum may well be called a "hero" of the Administrative Age. In every corporation that expands and integrates different operations into an efficient whole, there are similar heroes of administration who are not likely to be given the credit they deserve. They key factor, however, is that administrative process and efficiency served the purpose of growth as allies to the building and exploring process.

There is danger in this success. Robert McNamara, one of the "Whiz Kids," heroes of World War II, who enabled the logistical miracle that was performed by the United States military at that time, a miracle that created four complete new generations of aircraft to be designed, produced, and flown in battle within a four year period, came to believe that administrative control was synonymous with good management. He then became CEO of Ford Motor Company and imposed the dominance of accounting and control that diminished the innovation of engineers and destroyed any remaining social unity in the organization. He then took the same flawed mindset to the military as Secretary of Defense as we went to war in Vietnam. The results were disastrous.

The wealth profile is at its best and most balanced as the organization enters the Administrative Age. As it drifts toward bureaucracy, it again becomes out of balance. During this period the financial assets are growing, brand equity is increased, and human capital is increasing with the capacity to produce. It is likely that spiritual capital is the first resource that will decline during this period, followed by the loss of innovation and then internal sociability and trust. These losses are the leading indicators of decline.

You may be an Administrator if...

- You developed your career in the corporation's staff functions.
- You consider yourself expert at the procedures, processes and systems of management.
- Order, consistency, and smooth operations are high priorities for you.
- You devote more time to checking on what has happened, as reflected in financial and other reports, than you spend focused on future growth in products, services, or customers.

Your organization may be in the Administrative Age if...

- Much of the energy of the managers is devoted to streamlining and improving procedures.
- You are well established in your market and feel confident that customers will continue to buy from you.
- There is little sense of urgency or crisis.
- Your organization is investing in expensive offices and staff headquarters.
- New products or services are expected to come from the staff research and development group.

THE AGE OF THE BUREAUCRAT: THE TIGHT GRIP OF CONTROL

> *"The piper who has lost his cunning can no longer conjure the feet of the multitude into a dance; and if, in a rage and panic, he now attempts to turn himself into a drill sergeant or a slave-driver, and to coerce by force a people whom he feels that he can no longer lead by his old magnetic charm, then, all the more surely and more swiftly, he defeats his own intention; for the followers who had merely flagged and fallen behind as the heavenly music died away will be stung by a touch of the whip into active rebellion."* Arnold Toynbee

The transition from the Administrative Stage to that of the Bureaucrat occurs without any plan or intention. Old age happens. It needs no encouragement. No one in the history of organization ever created a design team to design and implement bureaucracy.

As soon as the leader imposes increasing levels of control in his love for order, he becomes a *bureaucrat* and loses understanding of the original organizing principle that was the energy created by the "word," the creative act that was the reason to unite and sacrifice. Now the lack of creativity leads to impotence in the marketplace, and survival is dependent on cost cutting and control and anyone with the creative spirit, potential Prophets who possess the very cure that is so needed are driven to exile or crucified for their violation of order. The decline will soon lead to death. The bureaucracy causes the exile or execution of those who are creative but unable to conform to the required order. With the departure of creativity, the fate of the company is sealed

In 30 A.D. Crassus the moneylender became head of the legions of Rome. H.G. Wells, the historian, said, "After the fall of Carthage the Roman imagination went wild with the hitherto unknown possibilities of finance. Money, like most other inventions, had "happened" to mankind, and men had still to develop – today they have still to perfect – the science of morality and money. What happened to Rome? Various answers are made – a decline of religion, a decline from the virtues of the Roman forefathers, and the like. We, who can look at the problem with a larger perspective, can see that what had happened to Rome was *money*. Money had floated the Romans off the firm ground."[19] And *money happens* to companies as the accountant becomes CEO and the focus and expertise at the top is on counting and recording and the maintenance of order and not on the engineering of the new car or the challenge of conquering a new market. This is the signal of decline in the company. This is the loss of creativity.

While financial assets are at their peak during this period, the spiritual and social forms of capital are declining quickly. The primary characteristic of the Bureaucratic Age is a loss of social purpose resulting in a loss of unity. The layered classes of the structure fail to understand each other and are increasingly devoted to their own self-interests. The leaders divorce themselves from their followers. The work force proceeds to develop its own bureaucracy to protect it from the unresponsive leadership of the company. The social fabric begins to rip apart.

With the Bureaucratic Age comes the age of skepticism. The employees in the Bureaucratic organization begin to doubt their leaders have a clear vision of the organization's future. They begin to doubt the value of dedicating their career to a company that appears to care little about them. The managers are beginning to doubt their own strategies as they increasingly are pushed  to make financial sense out of a less and less innovative response to the marketplace. Now they seek salvation in a mirage of unfamiliar enterprises or products. Perhaps there is more money in credit default swaps or mortgage backed securities, and the more they go astray from that which they know, the more they are taking

---

[19] Wells, H.G. *The Outline of History*. Garden City, New York. Doubleday & Company, Inc. 1971. pp. 385-86.

increasing risk with the financial assets of the company. They do not yet understand that the problem is not with the business, but with them.

Research has shown that retired persons, who have lost a sense of purpose and are no longer working to achieve some good outside of themselves, deteriorate both mentally and physically. The bureaucratic corporation is doing precisely the same thing.

In the Bureaucratic Age the members of the organization spend their declining energies not on innovation for customers, but on the struggle within. The more they focus on internal discord, the less they are capable of responding creatively to the challenges of the external environment. They now enter into more and more mergers and acquisitions, which increase the weight of the uncreative mass while reducing the number of creative leaders.

Leaders in this fifth stage of the life cycle begin to devote themselves to the symbols of their authority rather than the substance of the products and services in the marketplace. They build taller buildings; have larger and more grandiose offices, because these symbols talk to them. The symbols say "You are in charge. You do know what you are doing. You are an effective leader."

As the Administrator reduced the drive to innovation and expansion, the Bureaucrat must now increasingly focus on financial return. This is the period in time when investors are less likely to buy the company's stock because of its growth potential, but rather for its current dividend return and for security. This motive of shareholders then becomes the priority of the executives. More and more those shareholders are the customers rather than the buyers of products or services. The company is now about producing money, not about innovation. While not intending to create risk, the Bureaucrat is unwittingly creating the risk that will ultimately destroy the company. There is a shift from forward momentum to holding ground, and the need to produce financial returns increasingly drives out the potential of innovation and expansion that created the company's brand equity. The old lion is increasingly at risk of being beaten by young and aggressive competitors who see the weakness and are all the more willing to take the risk of attack.

This stage is the last chance for the organization. If it does not generate an internal revolution to refocus its energy and purpose, that revolution will be forced upon it by external events in the next stage.

The decline of corporations is often explained by pointing to external events such as foreign competition, new technologies, or changing economic or market conditions. Of course, these may have an influence. But the organization in balance is an adaptive mechanism. The job of leaders is to sense changing on the landscape and adjust their strategies to the new threats and opportunities that appear. The inability to make these adjustments, this loss of will, is the true reason for decline.

The decline of civilizations is similarly sometimes explained by external events, volcanoes, earthquakes, plagues, or the conquering barbarians. Arnold Toynbee analyzed the decline of twenty-three civilizations and rejected all of these explanations. H.G. Wells, the historian, examining the decline of Rome wrote:

"The two centuries of order between 27 B.C. and 180 A.D. may be counted as among the wasted opportunities of mankind. It was an age of spending rather than of creation, an age of architecture and trade in which the rich grew richer and the poor poorer and the soul and spirit of man decayed.

The Roman Imperial system... at its best had a bureaucratic administration which kept the peace of the world for a time and failed altogether to secure it... The clue to all of its failure lies in the absence of any free mental activity and any organization for the increase, development, and application of knowledge. It respected wealth and it despised science... It was a colossally ignorant and unimaginative empire. It foresaw nothing."

The defeat is a failure of creative leadership, but the leaders – either in civilization or corporations – are as much victims as they are criminals. Because of the numbers of layers below them, the information they receive is increasingly inaccurate and distorted. Because of the weight of the potential power they wield, their subordinates are less and less likely to confront them with the truth. This physical, intellectual, and spiritual separation between the leaders and the led is growing like a cancer undetected. And with this cancer, the group as a whole, is losing its ability to exert will.

The leaders of Lehman Brothers, Bear Sterns, and others were certainly intelligent and well knew the world of finance within which they operated. But somehow they were blind to the realities of what was happening within their own organizations and in their marketplace. Do you think that no one in the organization was aware that the mortgage backed securities they were trading had a real value far below that at which they were being sold and purchased? Did no one recognize that someone would eventually understand this discrepancy and a wave of selling would ensue? Of course there were those who understood this reality. But where were the minds of the leaders? In truth, they were behaving normally. They were victims of the bureaucracies and aristocracy that they themselves had created.

You may be a Bureaucrat if…

- You spend most of your time in meetings reviewing what has already happened or should have happened.
- You cannot remember when you last participated in the development of a new product or service… and, you don't think that's your job.
- You are more concerned with how you and your company are viewed by Wall Street analysts than by your customers.
- You believe tighter control will solve many of your organization's problems.
- You spend more time with central staff managers than with line sales and production managers and workers.

Your organization may be in the Bureaucratic Age if…

- Your company is growing more by acquisition than by internal new product creation.
- Your company has reorganized more than once in the past three years.
- You are more interested in the internal challenges of the organization than the external marketplace.
- Employees and managers alike feel that they can do little to alter the company's fortunes.
- Managers and employees tend to talk about the "good old days" when things were exciting and fun.

- Managing or fixing the systems and structure receives more time and attention than selling and producing.

THE AGE OF THE ARISTOCRAT: ALIENATION AND REVOLUTION

"Has God forgotten all I have done for him?" Louis XIV

"I hold that a little rebellion, now and then, is a good thing, and as necessary in the political world as storm in the natural environment." Thomas Jefferson

Management derives its power from its legitimacy, and in the Aristocratic Age legitimacy is lost. It is lost because the managers have stopped doing their job, that of leading, creating vision, and building unity of energy and effort across diverse people and interests. Peter Drucker said:

"Power has to be legitimate. Otherwise it has only force and no authority, is only might and never right. To be legitimate, power has to be grounded outside of itself in something transcending that is accepted as a genuine value... If power is an end in itself, it becomes despotism, both illegitimate and tyrannical."[20]

Legitimacy is a matter of perception, and it is the perceptions of the constituent groups that matter. In every relationship there must be a balance of power, a mutual concern, and respect. When these mechanisms break down, leadership acts on its own interests, and contrary to the interests of its followers; rebellion inevitably results.

The disintegration of culture may appear as either an internal revolution or an attack by a competing Barbarian. In either case, the cause is the same: the loss of social unity brought about by alienation of the leaders and their loss of legitimacy. It is not employees who become alienated from the leaders. It is leaders who have divorced their followers. They have moved to the 48th floor of the office tower and spent too much of their time surrounded by others who are striving to achieve the same level of

---

[20] Drucker, Peter. *The Frontiers of Management*: (New York: Truman Talley Books, E. P. Dutton, 1986), p. 180.

detachment from workers and customers. The more detached are the leaders, the more incapable they are of recognizing challenges and issuing forth a creative response to challenge. Woodrow Wilson understood:

"I do not believe that any man can lead who does not act, whether it be consciously or unconsciously, under the impulse of a profound sympathy with those whom he leads – a sympathy which is insight – and insight which is of the heart rather than of the intellect."

At this stage, the leader's focus, his motivation, has shifted from serving others to serving self. In the later days of a society, the leaders become obsessed with material self-gratification. This obsession is largely due to the loss of gratification normally derived from productive work. There is satisfaction to be derived from sawing and sanding wood into a piece of furniture, from designing, testing, and watching a mechanical object come to life, from listening to a customer and sincerely striving to meet his or her needs. All of these pleasures are lost to the Aristocrat. Now, the rewards come from the appearance of wealth. The irony is that the Aristocrat is not achieving greater satisfaction than a productive individual of modest resources. The supervisor whose team sets a new production record is undoubtedly achieving a higher level of satisfaction than the Aristocrat purchasing the Gulfstream IV or the new limousine or conducting grand meetings at a country club. The Aristocrat has been so long removed from productive work that he or she no longer remembers their satisfactions.

In all cases, revolutions are not started by the revolutionaries. Revolutions are started by Aristocrats who have abandoned their followers. Revolution is the response to the stimulus, and the stimulus is Aristocracy. Where unity of energy and effort was created by the Prophet, the Aristocrat has created alienation and division of social class. The theme is an old one: do you accept that a higher class has been granted the right to make decisions without accountability, or do you trust the "common people" to do what is right? Thomas Jefferson observed the two courses in society:

"Men by their constitutions are naturally divided into two parties: (1) Those who fear and distrust the people, and wish to draw all powers from them into the hands of the higher class. (2) Those who identify themselves with the people, have confidence in them, cherish and consider them as the most honest and safe. In every country these two parties exist; and in every one where they are free to think, speak, and write, they will declare themselves."

Both within companies and civilizations, the disintegration of a society is preceded by a period in which wealth is achieved by the manipulation of paper related assets, rather than by producing new assets. Some years ago, the writer Adam Smith pointed out:

"The Street money these days is made from pieces of paper – futures, options, tax shelters, moving corporate divisions from one balance sheet to another. That activity need not produce additional mousetraps. In the 1920s the games were played with utilities and holding companies. Pyramids were erected, companies owning companies owning companies, and the bootleg bubbly flowed until it all vanished."

Before the fall of Rome, before the fall of the stock market in 1929, and before the fall of Lehman and Bear Sterns, the senior executives were preoccupied not with the quality of a products, meeting customer needs, or developing innovative solutions, but with the cleverness of financial manipulations. It always accompanies Aristocracy, and it always ends in collapse and rebellion. The difficulty is that now our corporations and our economies are so intertwined that the failure of any major institution or economy pulls down the rest.

You may be an Aristocrat if...

- You manage an organization that has not successfully developed and marketed a new product or service for several years, and your only expectation for growth is through acquisition.
- Most of your time is spent on financial matters, strategic planning, and restructuring the organization, not with those who have their hands on producing or selling products or services.
- Your offices are plush with expensive artwork, you have limousine service, and you spend a lot of time at expensive social gatherings, for business, of course.
- You feel that only you and a small circle of advisers are capable of understanding the strategy of the corporation.

Your organization may be in the Aristocratic Age if...

- There is a complete separation in perception, expectations, and communication between those workers and managers who produce and sell and those who claim to be the leaders of the corporation.

- The leader thinks of himself (herself) as indispensible and almost synonymous with the company.

- A great deal of the time and energy is spent in internal warfare, both between horizontal units and vertical "classes."

- There is an almost constant process of reorganizing.

- There is a continual effort to cut costs, hold down wages, and the leaders are constantly warning of the gravity of the situation, yet their own compensation is increasing with no apparent relationship to the fate of the business.

RELATIVE WEALTH CURVES THROUGH THE LIFE CYCLE

Corporations, though of the same species, are very diverse animals. Some are born with a great deal of capital at the outset and search for a good idea to market. Others, more likely, are born with an inspiration, a marketable idea, and then search for capital, human resources and other requirements of growth. But, as they mature there are some relatively predictable, more common, relationships between the different forms of wealth, both in companies and civilizations. This illustration is intended to describe these general relationships. Spiritual Capital and innovation tend to be early capacities of the organization and as the weight of administration turns to bureaucracy, those forms of capital diminish rapidly. Social capital tends to build and begin to decline as the organization grows in size, but both internal and external sociability or trust can vary a great deal in their relationship to other forms of capital. It is normal that financial capital grows gradually and is at its peak during the age of the Administrator and Bureaucrat and then can decline with great rapidity. The ideal, of course, would be for each of these forms of wealth to reach some theoretical peak and then maintain that same level for a long period of time. That is most likely to occur if there is balance.

ACHIEVING BALANCE – THE SEARCH FOR THE FOUNTAIN OF YOUTH

Is it inevitable that growth and expansion are followed by bureaucracy and decline? If you study the course of civilization you might reach that conclusion as the long march of cycles appears as an inevitable pattern. But Arnold Toynbee asked himself this question some years after he wrote *A Study of History*. His answer was "no". He said that he believed in free will. He believed that if we understand the causes of integration and disintegration, of emergence and decline, we can alter our behavior and achieve an ever-advancing civilization. It is the failure to recognize and respond to new challenges that leads to a condition of ease, to the loss the power of self-determination, the loss of will.

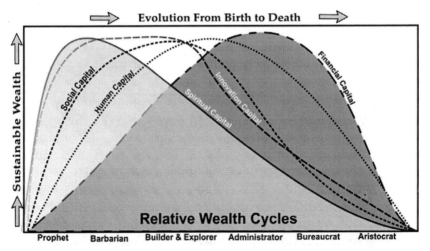

In human aging there are chemical biological processes over which we have no control. Of course, we can greatly influence human aging with diet, exercise, and our own social and mental activity. Organizations, on the other hand can be influenced even more. They are inherently capable of regeneration. Managers change, products change, the market changes, and all of these are opportunities for adaptation, and for adjusting the style, culture, and processes to prolong the life of the organization. The 3M Corporation has been through numerous periods of refocus, redefining its product portfolio, constantly innovating and maintaining its social capital within the organization and its brand equity. It is an "old" corporation that can act young. There are many other examples. And, of course there are examples of organizations that fail to adapt to new markets and technologies and become rigid and lose their ability to innovate within a very short period.

Revolution is the transformation brought about by leaders who recognize new challenges, acknowledge the failure to adapt to a changing landscape, and promote a new outlook, a new spirit, and new strategy. Corporations have proven that there is no fixed time frame of life cycles. The key to this success is always the ability to create synergy of the different styles or capabilities of leadership and to maintain a healthy balance of the five forms of wealth.

What are the lessons of this story? I think there are several. One is the diversity of leadership styles that are needed to fulfill the potential of any organization. As companies mature, the need for the creative Prophet does not disappear; nor does the need for the conquering spirit of the Barbarian. But what is needed is balance and the creation of synergy or harmony between the diversity of talents, each put to work on the challenges appropriate to the type of temperament. The most difficult of all tasks of leadership is to create unity from diversity. It is the purpose of a leadership team. On a leadership team you do not want ten Administrators who will create excellent and orderly plans but never have the energy to go anywhere. Nor do you want ten Barbarians, each with the strong will and singular focus to fight a battle. You also need the Builders, the engineers and specialists who know how to make complex things work and Explorers to expand the territory. And you need Administrators who bring order to complex organizations and tasks through counting and recording. But you do not need the excess of administration that is bureaucracy. You need leaders, or you need to become a leader, who can bring these personalities together in a harmonious orchestra.

Another lesson regards the role of personalities versus process and principles. Civilizations, when they have been at their peak, have had senates, election processes, systems of law, and separation of powers. When Rome was being born it was highly reliant on principles. This was the period, generally regarded as the peak of the civilization, when the Roman senate was supreme and the acceptance of Roman law and order prevailed. It then was overcome with cults and clashes of personality and the law became subservient to the personalities. The process of disintegration exactly paralleled the decline of the reliance on principles and process and the return of dominance of personalities.

INDEX